BREAKING
The
FIBRO CODE

Move from a Life of Pain to Possibility

BREAKING
The
FIBRO CODE

Move from a Life of Pain
to Possibility

Penny D. Chiasson, MS, CRNA, BCH

Disclaimer:

All session recollections are based on actual events. In order to maintain anonymity in ALL instances I have changed the names of individuals and places. I have also changed some identifying characteristics and details of the story such as occupation, gender, and circumstances. Every effort has been made to remove any likeness to the case being discussed.

Pain is a symptom our body provides us to let us know when we need to address a problem. This book nor the author cannot aid the reader in distinguishing acute from chronic pain, or pain which needs immediate medical attention. It is the responsibility of the reader to pay attention to their physical body and seek out appropriate medical attention and diagnosis when experiencing pain.

Praise For Breaking The Fibro Code

5 Stars

If you suffer from fibromyalgia, CRPS or other chronic pain, "Breaking the Fibro Code" is a necessary guide to reclaiming your life. As someone who has experienced chronic pain for several years, and have used ALL of the techniques in this book, I can tell you that they WORK. Just learning to pay attention to your self-talk and the stories you tell yourself about your body and your pain can have a huge impact on the way you feel.

Your perceptions and the way you think about your circumstances really does create your reality. I know that may seem like a strange idea to you right now. But I have experienced it and Penny is masterful in her techniques and the journey she guides you on throughout this book. So do yourself a favor and grab a copy for yourself and your loved ones, especially those suffering from debilitating chronic pain conditions.

Lisa P.

Confidence Coach, Online Visibility Expert,
Certified Consulting Hypnotist

5 Stars

"Breaking the Fibro Code: Move from a Life of Pain to Possibility" should be required reading for anyone diagnosed with chronic illness. Whether you've been newly diagnosed or managing chronic illness for years, you'll want to lean in as Penny shares how you can use the power of your subconscious mind to unlock your unique fibro code and fully enjoy your life.

Each chapter builds on the next, allowing you to build the foundation of transformation in your thinking and life.

I wish this book had been available to me when I was diagnosed in 2003 with chronic illness. The good news is it's here now and implementing Penny's suggestions has shifted my thinking and improved my quality of life. I'm no longer choosing to be a passenger in my life. I'm an active participant. I choose to work from a place of possibility and healing—I want the same for you."

Jennifer Laforet, Canada

5 Stars

Penny has gotten to know her reader, connect with them where they are and takes them on a journey of understanding how the subconscious and environment can be influenced to bring about healing which begins from the inside.

Thom Bloomquist, MSN, CRNA, CH, FAAPM; NH, USA

5 Stars

As a chronic pain sufferer , reading this opened my eyes , my mind and my heart to the fact that I will never be cured but it up to me to learn as much as I can about how to care for me! After reading this book I felt more positive about who I am and were I can go next! I felt so refreshed . The realization that so many people suffer the same way I do made me feel not so alone!

The knowledge I gained from this read will lead me on path to wholeness again! I have read many books about this issue and never once did I feel as positive as I did after reading this book! I feel so honored to have gotten to read this book. A huge thank you the author for all her hard work! I will recommend this book to non-sufferers! Good work! I love this!

Jacqueline Georget Vachon, Canada

5 Stars

"I really enjoyed reading "Breaking the Fibro Code." It was easy to read, and even though it is short, there is a lot to this book. Penny did an amazing job of explaining just how your mind influences the way your body adapts and develops disease. Her explanation prompted me to reflect back over my life and realize just how stealthy stress has become in my own life. There are tips in this book that I will definitely be using to maintain my own health and I will be sharing this book with friends. If you are on the fence about this book, just GET IT!"

L. Brandolini, CRNA; CT, USA

5 Stars

I have suffered with chronic pain for 12 years now, primarily with Fibromyalgia. I have searched trying to find ways to help with the pain. The book is packed with information for chronic pain and Fibromyalgia sufferers. At first is sounds real deep, but she explains it in such a way that it makes sense. Penny shows you how stress effects your pain & gives you ways to reduce your stress and in turn reduce your pain. I recommend this book to anyone that suffers with chronic pain and is ready to make some changes to improve their quality of life.

Debie L., Meridian, MS

5 Stars

"I was blown away by the introduction. I am so excited about the neuroplasticity concept. There is a lot more here than it seems. This book really grabbed my attention and it is a book I will read over and over again. Fibromyalgia had relegated me to a non-life. I no longer had vision or purpose. It has got to change and you have shown me how. This book is going to help a lot of people. It is already making differences in my everyday life and I hope to explore this further.

Kathleen H., USA

5 Stars

As a physician trained both chronic and acute pain management I can say there are many methods addressed in Mrs. Chiasson's book that are applicable in the management of chronic pain. Her book is written in an empathetic and conversational manner.

You will find honest encouragement & techniques based on her experiences with life and other patients that are practical for so many who deal with chronic pain."

John Bethea, MD

Associate Professor of Anesthesiology, Former President of Mississippi Society of Anesthesiologists, Chronic Pain Patient

---

5 Stars

In her book, "Breaking the Fibro Code: Move form a Life of Pain to Possibility," Penny Chiasson does a brilliant job of describing the origins of pain and the relationship between pain and the stress response. She clearly explains this relationship in a way that is easy for the reader to understand and identify with.

She outlines simple, mindful and hypnotic practices that offer the reader ways to reduce their own stress and in turn reduce their pain. This book is a must-read for anyone suffering from chronic pain, as well as professionals working with patients or clients of chronic pain.

Brad Tunis CH, MPA and Mindfulness Coach

---

5 Stars

This book is a must-read for anyone suffering from chronic pain! Eye-opening and inspiring, Penny shows you how to unleash your "secret" weapon and win your battle against pain. You are not simply a victim of your genes. Penny's practices and research prove that you can take your health back in ways that are simple, doable and fun.

Michelina C. DiSibio

Health & Prosperity Coach
www.lettucebethegood.com

5 Stars

This book is essential for anyone dealing with chronic illness or fibromyalgia. As someone who is also dealing with chronic illness, Penny has helped me connect the dots between our conscious awareness of illness and the subconscious influence on illness. In doing so, I feel empowered that I can use abilities I already have to unlock healing from within.

The mind-body techniques presented in this book will definitely change the life of the reader for the better. I strongly recommend this book to everyone!

Chuen Chuen Yeo

Leadership Agility Coach, ACEsence

Contents

Dedication

This is for you who knows the struggle of pain. They say it's all in your head, as though you are playing a game. You are seeking answers but find confusion instead. If someone would just listen, you might get ahead. Be fearless, seeking and mind open wide. Inside of you, your unique code resides. For within you there has always been everything you need to feel whole again. It's time; you're ready to take the reins, show them your power within.

Today the journey truly begins.
How will you show up..?
Today YOU have a CHOICE.
To question, to doubt, to resist...
Or...
To step in, to embrace, to flow...
Take a moment to BE present.
Inhale a breath and FEEL this feeling...
This stirring in your gut...
Only YOU can give it a name.
Only YOU allow it to matter.
Give yourself GRACE.
Find a moment of PEACE.
And remember to ENJOY the RIDE...
Your healing journey is a ride...
Not a race...
A ride
Into the unknown...
the stories, the identities, the beliefs...
A Journey into YOU...
into your Best Self...

~Jill Renee Stevens

Introduction

C hronic pain has become a crisis in our country. Physicians are overwhelmed and burnt out with the levels of chronic pain and illness they are seeing in a new healthcare environment that does not support taking time with the patient. Licensed healthcare professionals work to understand and treat chronic diseases such as fibromyalgia every day. The foundation of these diseases is complex. Because there is no one single identifiable cause and no one effective treatment, practitioners can become frustrated helping you find an effective solution.

This is why it is so challenging for providers when they are trying to help you. Fibromyalgia is a brain-based syndrome. You may experience many other ailments, along with fibromyalgia and chronic pain. It is not uncommon to see reflux disease, irritable bowel syndrome, neuropathy, migraines, skin issues, and many more symptoms that I don't have room to list here. I want you to know a diagnosis of fibromyalgia does not mean you have to suffer. You have options.

There is hope.

It is not hopeless. There are things that you can do, right now, to move circumstances in your favor. In this book, I am going to share with you research-proven techniques I use with all my chronic pain clients. Science supports these techniques. Because you are reading this book, I know that you are ready to do everything that you can to make a difference in your health. Use the tools I teach you here and work with your doctor. Your healing is a partnership. I am excited that you are ready to get into the game.

In 2009, I was standing in line at an airport at Guayaquil, Ecuador. I was heading to the Galapagos Islands as a team member of a medical mission. They were inspecting my bags for any item that might have seeds, chemicals, or plants. That included any piece of fruit or healthy raw nut you might have packed to eat. Each and every person, including the frocked Catholic priest going to the Galapagos Archipelago, had everything inspected. All "contraband" went into the trash to protect the internal sanctity and innocence of the environment of the islands.

Just one foreign seed, plant, chemical, or pest (yes, insects and animals included) could disrupt and destroy the entire ecosystem in the Galapagos. It did not stop with the inspection. Once we were on the plane and preparing for descent to the islands, the cabin of the aircraft was fumigated to eradicate anything that may be on our clothing.

Once we arrived on the island, we received a picture ID card that was similar to a visa. You had 100 days, and then you were out. They did not want people staying and changing the internal environment of the island.

What does this have to do with fibromyalgia you ask? Stay with me. This is very important. For you to understand why the information you are about to learn is so important, you should know the potential of your body to react to your environment, inside and out.

Imagine an individual cell in your body. It is an island. An island where limited foods grow and most of your supplies of food and nutrients have to go. Your cell has a membrane that controls the passage of what comes in and out. That membrane also has "locks" (receptors) that can be unlocked by "keys" (chemicals in the fluid outside of the cell) that turn on activities within the cell. Just like the Galapagos and its natural habitat, your cell functions at its best when its environment is as close to original as possible.

Protect your body like the beautiful island it is.

It is common to walk along the rocky shore or beaches of the Galapagos and walk within feet of a seal, blue-footed booby, or iguana. These animals have no predators. Startling them, feeding them, or any other direct interaction is forbidden to protect the innocence of the island.

Now imagine that the government changed the rules, and this was no longer a protected space. Visitors are allowed to stay as long as they like, run around treating the wildlife like Disney™ characters, and bring foreign fruits and plants on the island that could grow wild and unchecked.

At first, it may seem like no big deal. A few plants, a few tourists…

what's the problem? Within a few years, this environment begins to change. Foreigners are allowed to move to the islands with all of their worldly habits. This pristine natural environment becomes lost to pollution. The unchecked growth of plants that don't belong continues, strangling out the native plants and leaving the animals without their natural food sources.

The same thing happens inside your body's cells. The function of your cells is determined by the environment outside of it and what it has available to make those important processes happen. Just like the airport inspectors, the cell membrane works to keep out harmful chemicals. However, let's say that the "gateway'" or "lock" was changed, and harmful substances or too much of something that is not usually harmful was allowed in. It would overwhelm the environment inside the cell.

Now the cell becomes stressed (cellular stress, oxidative stress) as the internal environment changes. The cell has a nucleus (the capital of the island), and it activates departments (genes) to deal with the state of emergency. Your genes are turned on and off by cellular activation of DNA.

Now, the islands are a part of a larger country (your body). If there were a natural disaster or manmade disaster (financial or environmental), the supply chain of foods and goods available to the island might change. Your brain (and gut membrane) control the environment of your body.

When you experience emotional, mental, or physical stress, the brain adjusts your environment based on primitive survival mechanisms. It is all unconscious. Your brain works to adapt and keep you safe. To do this, it *learns*.

If your brain created it, your brain can change it.

A process called neuroplasticity allows the brain to place meaning on what is going on inside and outside of you. Every thought, feeling, and human interaction create a response, and then the brain gives it meaning. You will soon learn that subconsciously, the brain is constantly sifting through these events and comparing your current environment to them so it can protect you by kicking your primitive stress system into action.

This brain-based mechanism (primarily) and what we bring into our body via the gut influences the cellular environment. It is primarily internal stressors within the brain that trigger fibromyalgia. It could be stress due to a physical injury, surgery, a post-traumatic stress-causing event, or chronic activation of the stress response from our emotional environment.

When our mind is hurting, we do not see rashes. It does not itch or bruise (it can, but not in this case) to let us know. It does something else to get our attention. It creates pain. Pain is a symptom that something is wrong. It can take months or years to get a diagnosis of fibromyalgia because pain is a symptom of so many different injuries and diseases.

Pain is a symptom. I know it is frustrating for you to hear, but even if you have a broken arm, pain is a symptom letting you know that there is a problem. Pain is an alarm signal when there is something wrong. That "something wrong" can be physical, chemical, or even emotional in origin. Fibromyalgia and chronic pain research in these areas confirm this.

Over time, if a person doesn't address the cause of the brain-based activation, the long-term chronic stress has adverse effects on the cells. As a result, secondary problems (autoimmune disease, metabolic disorders, irritable bowel syndrome, myofascial pain syndrome, etc.) occur due to the chronic inflammation that existing in the body. Things like poor diet, irregular sleep-wake cycle, and lack of physical activity make the situation worse. If you don't take measures soon to interrupt this cycle, the body will continue to adapt to it the best it can.

The cells adapt through epigenetic expression, and those adaptations are not always helpful. It is what the cells need to do to survive the stress. One thing that almost all the research has in common is the identification of epigenetic expression in chronic pain. New blood tests that have come on the horizon that identify activated genes have created understandable confusion. Leading people to believe that the problem lies in their genes and they have no choice is simply untrue.

Dozens of studies identify changes in the expression of specific genes as a result of relaxation training and other mind-body techniques. Genes can be turned on or off positively enhancing health and the body's ability to adapt and sometimes reverse illness. Some of the genes affected are involved in antioxidant production and cellular regeneration (cellular healing).

We only use a very tiny fraction of the genes with which we are born. Genes within our body become activated at the cellular level, depending on their environment. The beautiful thing about epigenetics is that genes that help us to heal or to improve our health and our body's functioning can be turned on in the same way as genes that cause us illness and disease.

Earlier, I mentioned neuroplasticity, which happens before epigenetic expression. This is why many people with fibromyalgia will seek out genetic testing and receive a "negative" result. Neuroplasticity is simply a fancy word meaning that the brain is relearning by creating new pathways. The wonderful thing about neuroplasticity — you can retrain your brain. That's simply all it is; training the brain in a new way to think and feel. Neuroplasticity is one of the ways that hypnosis can be so effective in helping people to release stress, fear, anxiety, and even chronic pain. If you use the tools I am going to teach you as early in the process as possible, you might be able to prevent epigenetic expression.

Just because it is simple doesn't make it easy.

Merely learning new ways to think about yourself, your diagnosis, and what it all means has been proven in the research to decrease discomfort and suffering, plus reduce symptoms of depression and anxiety. It is proven, but all this research in the hands of everyday practitioners can sometimes be too much. Some of the earlier research is conflicting, and new studies are published every day.

Your doctors do their best to keep up with the most recent research on hundreds of diseases they manage. That's why key concepts like exercise, stress, and emotional trauma stand out to them. Your doctors and nurse practitioners care and do their best for you. However, they also want to empower you with knowledge to care for yourself.

That's why you may hear statements (and I'm not making excuses here, this is unacceptable) like "it's all in your head," "you just need to get stress out of your life," "you just need to exercise more," or the most insulting of all, "you just need to be more positive." It's hard enough that friends and family may look at you and sees someone who, on the outside, has no apparent physical injury. You have to deal with their judgments and attitudes that you're "faking it" or "just too damn lazy." Then you may have to face a doctor, whose only answer is 'you have to live with it.' This is simply untrue.

As you continue reading through this book, I will draw from experiences with many clients that I have worked with for their chronic pain. Each client started in a different place. Every client had their unique symptoms. Each client had their unique results. This book will introduce you to the concepts that I use when working with clients so that we can tease out the areas that impact their life the most. This information helps us unlock their unique code to comfort.

Are you ready to move from pain to a life of possibility?

It is my intention that this book will guide you through a process of discovery of how you can gain control of one facet of your body's ability to turn on its healing mechanism, and that whether you believe it or not, you will embrace it and run with it. After all, it doesn't cost you anything unless you don't try.

I know that many of you are going to say, "This doesn't work; I've tried that."

"For how long?" I ask. My response is your fibromyalgia and chronic pain did not come into existence overnight. Neither will its reversal.

Others have done it. I already know you have the determination to be better. If you didn't have that determination to be better, you wouldn't be going from doctor to doctor to doctor looking for answers, yearning to be free of the pain that is robbing you of your future.

It's not impossible because if you're like me, you have been in fibromyalgia support groups across Facebook and other platforms. You have seen stories every day of someone who said, "Enough is enough. I'll do whatever it takes because my destiny is greater than this." And they do it!

I challenge you to love yourself, to be open with yourself, and to open your mind to the dream desire and possibility that you can live your life more comfortable. You can get more out of life. You can sleep better, have more energy, and once again be in control. I ask you to continue reading with an open mind of moving from a life of pain to one of possibility.

"Health is a state of complete harmony of the body, mind, and spirit. When one is free from physical disabilities and mental distractions, the gates of the soul open."

– B.K.S. Iyengar

CHAPTER 1

You are MORE than your Genes

"Whether you believe you can or you believe
you can't, you are probably right."

— Henry Ford

Chronic pain is useless. I don't have to tell you that. It is also complex, and there is no "one size fits all" answer to it. As I have worked with hundreds of people, their problems created an internal conflict within me as to what I could do to help them. Our current healthcare system does not allow us to focus on the whole body, mind, and spirit to neutralize the root cause of the problem. As a result, I set out on a journey to build a systematic approach to unlocking your personal healing code. This prompted me to do extensive research and go through my notes and interview my clients. My observations show that chronic pain is a systemic problem. Fortunately, you can move through this simple process to discover the key to unlocking your personal healing code. That's what you'll learn about in this book.

Pain itself activates your stress response. If you experience pain, your automated stress response is activated.

Specifically, you'll learn how to activate a chemical response in the body that decreases inflammation, creates relaxation, and enables a healing response in the body. You'll also find out how to recognize external triggers that affect your health and well-being mentally, physically, and emotionally. You'll even discover simple ways to take back control of your life. All of this allows your brain's chemistry to tip from one of chronic, subconscious stress activation to one of restoring health.

"Balancing the stress response and decreasing the inflammatory response may decrease the [pain] sensitization seen in fibromyalgia and other chronic pain syndromes."[1]

John is coming in to see what can be done about his chronic pain. He is a musician and has experience with hypnosis and knows it works. John used hypnosis to reprogram his brain when he experienced dystonia, a condition where neural pathways for muscles used repetitively can stop working. One of his fingers would no longer function when he played the trumpet. John created new neural pathways so he could play by using hypnosis and visualization.

It's truly one of my favorite and most exciting moments. I'm about to chat with John about his struggles with chronic pain. Doctors told him that there's nothing that can be done for the pain other than to have injections and hope they work. He's bringing in a note signed by his doctor saying that there's not something more serious going on. The last thing I want to do is mask someone's pain that could be a symptom of a serious problem.

Every time I take on a new client, I like to talk to them about the issues surrounding their discomfort. John arrives at the front, and I go out to meet him. We walk back to my office. He's visibly in significant discomfort. I note it in his gait. The very first part of our consult is the most important. It is my intention that John knows that I'm listening, that what he says matters, and that I care. After hearing John's story, I ask a few more questions to tease out any subconscious cues of the direction we need to take.

Once I know that John knows that I'm on his side, I begin to explain to him my process. I lightly touch on a few of the concepts in this book, but not in too much detail. I know I can help John if he will partner with me in the process to take back control of discomfort. One of the things that I do talk about with John is the role of the body's stress mechanism in amplifying discomfort. I want him to be armed with some knowledge whether he chooses to work with me or not.

Knowledge is power, but only if you use it!

I'm going into more detail here on the role of stress and its role in chronic pain. You are in a different place than everyone else reading this book. So, even if you are aware of this connection, I encourage you to read this chapter to the end. I wrote it anticipating possible questions or the desire to truly know more. I really go to the heart of the matter because knowledge is power when you use it.

In the following paragraphs, you might feel a little frustrated or even a little irritated at me at times. Cuss at me, throw the book, and get it out of your system. I want you to know I'm not here to judge you; I'm here to give you your power back. I'm telling you things that every doctor you have ever seen should have explained to you in detail so that you can maintain a state of health instead of sickness. I know you are sick and tired of being sick and tired.

We have normalized stress in our lives. We no longer recognize it.

One of the most frustrating things to hear is for your doctor to say you need to get stress out of your life. "Relax more, go exercise," they say, or even worse, "Well, you're gonna hurt the rest of your life. Get used to it." No one knows what your day is like but you. Maybe you experience stressful situations in your life. Maybe you don't. Maybe the stress is out of your control. Or maybe you haven't recognized how stealthy stress is and how it has crept into your everyday routine, and like hundreds of millions of people, you don't know it yet. A busy life with deadlines, school activities, political chaos, and media that bombards you with dramatic headlines almost hourly has become the norm. Stress has become the norm.

> *"...decreased cortisol levels from chronic stress activation are well documented and linked to pain disorders like fibromyalgia, chronic fatigue syndrome, chronic pelvic pain and TMJ disorders."*[2]

Over several decades, the role of stress in illness has become common knowledge in the health care community. From ulcers to heart attacks, illness has been blamed on a Type A personality since the 1970s. These are the most common examples, and they are dangerous. This stereotype of what stress is and what it does misleads a lot of people.

Stress can be both good and bad.

Imagine you are driving, and children are playing up ahead. Your subconscious is aware of the potential danger. It starts firing the stress response to sharpen your vision and quicken your reflexes. A child steps off the curb, and you quickly react. That is your stress response in action. During that time, your automated stress response also activated your immune system and other factors to protect you in the event of physical injury. This is a situation where stress is good.

Now, think about buying a new house. You love the house, and you feel that it is meant to be yours. You are excited about being a home-owner, the bidding process, and finding out the house is yours. This is good, but it can still create short-term stress. Then, six weeks later, your job security becomes uncertain. Things are changing faster than you can adapt. You have a cold (which you rarely have), and now headaches seem to be an everyday thing. Weeks become months of worry. You lose your job. Unemployment doesn't pay the mortgage. What are you going to do? How will you survive? This is a pattern of chronic stress that is bad stress.

Your conscious mind can only process 7–9 bits of information. The subconscious can process 7 TRILLION.

Stress is anything that puts key areas of the brain on alert. Your brain is wired to keep you safe and in a steady state. You can experience stress without even knowing you are stressed. It is automatic. Any time your subconscious (note I did not say you) detects fear, uncertainty, or that you are stepping out of your normal routine, it can activate the Automated Stress Response in the body. Short-term stress preps the body for fight or flight. Chronic stress can wreak havoc on the body, and your body's response to stress will be unique.

It's not your genes; it's their environment.

Now, you may be thinking that if all of this is subconscious, you are unable to control any of it. Just like your DNA, right? Nothing could be further from the truth. Our health is more than our DNA. We are more than our DNA, environment, relationships, and lifestyle. We are a complex masterpiece made up of a delicate dance between all of these. Scientists are publishing research every day that proves this to be true. That is why a one size fits all approach to your pain and health rarely works. That's why when someone tells you "it's in your genes" or to "just live with it" they are wrong. You have to break your code.

It is important to learn and break your code because up to 90% of all doctor's visits are for stress-related symptoms. If you are like most people, you do not realize just how many symptoms you experience that are related to stress. It is amazing how our most basic survival mechanism can create illness and discomfort—that which it is designed to protect us from!

Again, small amounts of stress are healthy. It boosts our immune system and preps our body for survival. Most people will experience a mild case of nerves such as mild stomach upset, heartburn, flushing, sweaty palms, and jitters. These are all a result of the automatic stress response.

Chronic stress is going to lead to more serious problems. It can be a long, slow process, or brought on by an illness or physically/emotionally traumatic event. You might be completely unaware of when and where it all started.

Disease presents at the weakest link

Think of your body's systems as links of a chain. When there is no tension, there is no stress on the links. They are solid and at ease. When tension is applied to one end of the chain, but not on the other, the links are still solid and at ease. When tension is applied at both ends, the chain loses its slack. It is no longer at ease. If the tension applied is strong enough, or the construction of the chain has a weakness, the chain will begin to give. The tension can be intermittent or constant.

One end of the chain is attached to internal stress. Internal stress is created by fear, excitement, uncertainty, memories, and incomplete tasks (more on this later). The other end of the chain is made up of external stress like work environment, crowded commutes, nutrition, relationships, and environment. The makeup of the chain links is in our DNA and influenced by genetics and epigenetics. The key word being influenced, not controlled.

The automated stress response by the autonomic nervous system and the HPA axis both result in the release of adrenaline and noradrenaline (fight or flight chemicals that restrict blood flow, increase heart rate and conversion of fat to glucose (sugar).

The automated stress response sets off a chemical response in the body that affects all of the systems. It does this through two pathways. The first is called the autonomic nervous system (ANS); the second is the hypothalamic-pituitary-adrenal (HPA) axis or the cortisol response. The names are not as important as understanding how they are affecting your body. The ANS causes the following when activated: increased blood pressure, increased heart rate, slowed digestion, sweating, increased glucose release into the blood, dilated pupils, and diverted blood flow to large muscle groups. The HPA axis or cortisol response is activated, which helps the body maintain a sustained stress response by releasing adrenaline, noradrenaline, and cortisol. A few seconds of stress activates the HPA axis for hours.

Cellular (oxidative) stress and the Automated Stress Response are linked

Chronic activation of the automated stress response can result in changes in the brain itself. It becomes less sensitive to feedback that should shut off the stress response. Stress hormones affect gene expression leading to disease. It alters the balance and function of digestion, immune function, inflammation, nervous system function, pain perception, and mental well-being. Chronic activation of inflammation plays a huge role in your comfort and overall well-being.

As a result of chronic activation, we see diseases like heart disease, type 2 diabetes, irritable bowel syndrome, myofascial pain syndrome (also known as Tension Myositis Syndrome), asthma, obesity, headaches, depression, anxiety, sleep dysfunction, and hundreds of other conditions. Every day, people reverse their diabetes, IBS, TMS, and other stress-related disorders by learning to identify and eliminate stress activation.

"Chronic stress has significant effects on the immune system that can ultimately manifest an illness."[3]

Small studies now suggest we may be able to minimize symptoms or possibly even reverse (if caught early enough) diseases like fibromyalgia, rheumatoid arthritis, lupus, and MS by learning to alter our stress response. Researchers have called for larger studies. You may be

7

genetically predisposed to a condition, but if you can prevent the expression of the gene or the neuroplastic changes that activate the condition, you will not experience it.

Stop inflammation in its tracks

Epigenetics is the study of how cellular gene expression is activated and how it affects your body. The role of stress in chronic pain is well documented, and there is research linking epigenetic changes in the immune system and inflammation to chronic pain. The good news is that we can activate a relaxation response in the body that stops inflammation in its tracks. That's right. Research demonstrates how we can activate the counter mechanism in real-time to bring our system back into alignment.

Activation of this mechanism costs nothing, and is available to you 100% of the time.

Adopt an attitude of curiosity

Within you is the ability to activate and manipulate your body's balance of stress and hormones in your favor. Simply accepting this possibility and adopting an attitude of curiosity about pushing your body's chemical balance towards health and comfort is the first step in reducing internal stress.

John and I had three sessions together. The first, four days before an injection, one the morning of the injection, and another two days after. After our first hypnosis session together and teaching John techniques to reduce external stress influencing his discomfort, he had a phenomenal weekend. He said it was so easy to get in and out of the car, and for the first time in a long time, he got out of bed without any discomfort. I always reassess my clients, so I honed in on getting out of bed without discomfort.

John said, "Usually, the discomfort is not when I first get out of bed but when I lie back down, and I get up the second time. I asked him what happened between the first time he got out of bed and the second time. He replied, "I watched the news."

So I asked, "How does the news make you feel, John?"

He replied, "It pisses me off."

I looked at him with my head tilted and one eyebrow cocked. I smiled with approval when I saw the light bulb visibly go off on his face. That day, he adopted a new practice of not watching the news on TV before he got out of bed. That afternoon he went for his injection and was told it would be about two weeks before he would receive any relief. When I saw him on his follow-up two days later, he was 100% pain-free, and at last check, he remains so.

You are Destined to be Something MORE!

Let me emphasize the critical point, simply because it's so important: Your body is complex, and so is the way all its systems interconnect in their response to stress, and thus creating symptoms ranging from pain to itching to inflammation to immune dysfunction. What's more, your body's response is not going to be identical to anyone else. You are UNIQUE. Here's what I suggest you do next: Make a list of all of your symptoms. Then make a list of all stressors you can identify in your life right now. So, go ahead and get started right away. The sooner you can identify the small changes you can make in your life to make a big impact, the better!

Once you move from understanding to knowing, you can put the power of your mind to work for you.

Move Forward!

List all of the stressors you can think of and find three that you can eliminate today. Then head over to Facebook and join my free community Breaking the Fibrocode to meet other fibro conquerors who have put themselves into the driver's seat of life.

Examples: news, Facebook, gossip, kids, illness, money issues, sick parents, elderly parents, traffic, work stress, major deadlines, unnecessary deadlines, moving, things you feel you SHOULD do, but life wouldn't change if you did not.

https://facebook.com/groups/thefibrocode

"True silence is the rest of the mind, and is to the spirit what sleep is to the body, nourishment, and refreshment."

William Penn

CHAPTER 2

Yin And Yang of Health

"To keep the body in good health is a duty... otherwise we shall not be able to keep our mind strong and clear."

Buddha

Knowing where to start is a growing problem for chronic pain sufferers. Fortunately, however, fibro conquerers like you don't have to suffer from information overload once you know how to pinpoint specific areas where you can focus your attention.

That's what you'll learn about in this chapter. Specifically, you will learn how to begin shifting from a state of stress activation to chemical relaxation by becoming aware of your thoughts. You'll also find out how to activate your vagus nerve naturally. You'll even discover how to hack your to-do list to reduce stress. So, without further introduction, let's jump in with a discussion of how reducing anxiety and overthinking can have a significant impact on the way your body responds.

As I sat at my desk with my office door open, Gwen came hurrying in. "Penny, I need your help!" Gwen worked in the office next door, and we had developed a professional relationship over the previous year. Gwen continued to tell me that she was scheduled to have surgery soon, and she was very nervous. You see, Gwen experiences severe nausea and vomiting with any pain medications, and anesthesia made it worse.

Relaxation techniques can decrease pain during and after surgery.

I spent a few minutes talking to Gwen about what she could do to minimize any issues by decreasing her stress response. I explained how stress could make all of these symptoms worsen, and worry creates stress. Once she got it, I gave her relaxation hypnosis to listen to in the two weeks prior to surgery. I also gave her a CD her anesthesia provider could play through headphones while she was under anesthesia.

> *"50% of missed workdays and 75% of doctor visits are due to stress…emotional stress is a major contributing factor to deaths from cardiac and respiratory disease."[4]*

Interrupting the stress response (what I call the Yang of health) is about more than the elimination of stress because all stress cannot be eliminated. To experience the benefits, you need to activate your relaxation response. For Gwen, the relaxation CD was a major part of her success. She was not sleeping because she was worried. Worry is negative thinking. In a focused state, this worry becomes negative subconscious suggestion.

Negative thoughts are a form of stress

Every single thought we have creates a neurochemical response in the brain. Thoughts, memories, and even the imagination trigger emotion in the subconscious mind (SCM). The SCM also takes this information to determine our overall state of being (am I safe, am I in danger). The interpretation of these thoughts by the SCM triggers feedback to the hypothalamus. The hypothalamus can then activate (or not) the automated stress response system.

You might be asking what is the point of knowing a thought can activate the stress response? You may be saying to yourself that it is really no big deal, but it is. Our instinctual protection mechanism cannot tell the difference between small everyday stress and a bear chasing you through the woods.

"Increased positive emotions build physical health by increasing vagal tone. Positive emotion and positive social connections create a sustainable positive spiral with physical health."[5]

As our modern lives have evolved, our physical bodies have not. Constant deadlines, overloaded schedules, social media notifications, or the inability to escape work due to mobile email accounts put us under constant stress. We have normalized it in our lives, so we don't even realize it is happening. It is why we must take action now to bring balance back to the Yin and Yang of our health, and to go one step further to tip the scales to Yin.

You were created to live in a state of peace

Gwen popped back into my office two days before her surgery. She was surprised and excited because, finally, just the night before, she listened to the CD. "I slept last night for the first time in weeks. I should have started listening before last night!" I encouraged her to listen on her lunch break, before bed for the next two days, and the morning of surgery to maximize the effects.

When Gwen used the CD, she interrupted her stress response and activated her relaxation response. When she followed the hypnosis, she stopped thinking. When she stopped thinking, it cut off all of the negative inputs into the brain. Then in more mentally relaxed states of hypnosis, the relaxation response becomes activated. The heart rate slows, breathing slows, and the body takes a break. She tipped her body's Yin and Yang toward a balance of relaxation and healing.

Our bodies are designed to live in this state of relaxation. We are wired to thrive in love, gratitude, and happiness. The term "relaxation response" should be reconsidered. It should be called the "vitality response." Because in reality, this state of vitality is supposed to be our normal baseline. The stress response is there for immediate survival. The vitality response is for living a full and enjoyable life.

Think of all the pleasures you enjoy. Lungs full of fresh air. Healthy, glowing skin. Abundant energy. Great food. Loving relationships. Intimate satisfaction. A focused mind. These are just a few of the areas in life that our vitality is responsible for.

The YIN of health is carried out by the vagus nerve

While the stress response system is made up of many, many nerves and a backup system to keep it supercharged, your relaxation response is maintained by one nerve. References to the vagus nerve are now appearing everywhere it seems. It is interesting to me, simply because Dr. Herbert Benson uncovered the value in naturally stimulating this nerve in the 1970s. He is responsible for coining the phrase "relaxation response," and Harvard has an institute in Dr. Benson's name dedicated to relaxation response research.

There are a lot of possible reasons that this is only now gaining intense focus. However, I only want to focus on one. Epigenetics. Chronic pain, which originates in the brain, is a result of changes in genetic expression. The cause of this genetic expression is the chemical environment around the cells, forcing adaptation. Chronic exposure to stress depletes the effect's stress response and reduces cortisol levels. This causes low levels of chemicals that enhance the brain's ability to reduce pain.

Recent studies demonstrate that through natural activation of the vagus nerve, cortisol levels begin to normalize, and awareness of pain decreases. This is one piece of a very complex puzzle that makes up your unique code.

Naturally decrease your pain sensitivity

Modern media and medicine have conditioned us to expect a medication or treatment to yield results quickly. Everything in our current daily lives creates a subconscious desire for immediate gratification. This creates even more stress. Are you beginning to see the cycle here? The first step in succeeding is to let go of quick results. Commit to a process of taking control of your overall health.

There is a component of naturally creating relief that you cannot overlook. That is the consistency of use. It can take the brain and body days to weeks of repetitive practice of mind-body techniques to create change in the body. Why? The body has to recognize it's new chemical environment is consistent. Then it will begin the process of resetting and activating cells (epigenetics again) to adjust.

You are a natural-born healer

Many diseases experienced today are brought on by the chemical environment created by stress in the body. Most of them you have heard of and maybe even experienced. Almost all of them have been noted to exist along with fibromyalgia. Scientific study and research supports and records the reversal of many of these disease states through stress-reduction and activation of the vitality response.

Take diabetes, for instance. Insulin resistance (pre-diabetes) and type 2 diabetes are a result of epigenetic gene activation. The research proves this can be reversed through stress modulation. Asthma is another stress-related condition. Chronic stress activation leads to an overactive inflammatory response. Stress modulation using natural vagus stimulation has strong, anti-inflammatory effects.

"Anything that tips the balance to the parasympathetic response [increases vagal tone] will improve prognosis in [cardiac risk]."[6]

Lifestyle modifications that improve [stress activation] balance:

Exercise

Social Support

Faith/Spirituality

Medication

Normal Sleep Patterns

Weight loss

Smoking Cessation

Stress Reduction

Curtis and O'Keef, 2002.[7]

When we have adequate vagal tone, our body is in a state to allow natural healing to occur. It also will enable genes associated with healing and optimum health to be active. Our bodies were created to heal themselves. When you get a cut, it heals. Minor infections heal. Sprained muscles repair themselves. You don't have to tell your body how to do it. There is no pill that heals muscles and cuts. We survived thousands of years before modern medicine was born.

Start breaking even

How many times has your doctor told you to reduce your stress? It seems an impossible task at times. The two easiest ways are to eliminate negative thinking and worry. But what if you are in a situation that you cannot change? We will address that later. First, I want to make you aware of the ways you might be creating stress in your life that you do not realize.

Are you creating unrealistic expectations for yourself? When you have a good day, are you trying to get everything done, so you feel accomplished? This creates unnecessary stress that you may be unaware of. By having a long list of small tasks, or a short list of some very big projects, you might easily overexert yourself. In the moment, you might not feel it, but the next day you could be fatigued or sore. When you have things that need to be done, make a list. Divide the list into daily tasks and projects. Then break the projects down into steps. Every time you complete a step, check it off the list. This trick creates a sense of satisfaction and completion in the brain. It reduces stress, especially when you cannot complete the entire project.

Next, interrupt negative thinking. Negative thoughts create a negative sense of well-being. It can be a negative thought about your health, a memory from the past, or worry about a future that we cannot predict. By recognizing these thoughts and shifting your attention, you interrupt the activation of the stress response. To start, allow yourself to begin to recognize when you have a negative thought. Then shift your attention somewhere else. Start doing this now. As we will discuss later, our thoughts become habits. To heal, we need to become a master of our thoughts.

Create Positive Balance

One of the most basic things we have forgotten how to do is breathe properly. When we breathe properly, vagus nerve endings in the lungs and abdomen are stimulated. This sends information back to the brain and down to the heart. The vagus nerve sends and receives information influencing heart rate and blood pressure.

"Deep slow breathing increased tolerance to bone pain and increased gastric motility [i.e., gastroparesis]."[8]

Proper breathing is called diaphragmatic breathing or pranayama in yoga. Proper breathing not only influences the heart rate and blood pressure. Vagal activation promotes an anti-inflammatory chemical release. It allows cortisol levels to return to normal levels. Cortisol helps the brain effectively block pain awareness, and the anti-inflammatory chemicals block the pain amplification of inflammation. In chapter 3, I will teach you how to take a proper breath.

Other ways to stimulate your vagus nerve is to sing or laugh. When you find a favorite song and take those nice deep breaths to belt out a long note, or even enjoy a great belly laugh, you stimulate the nerve.

"Stimulation of stomach vagal afferents [nerve endings] stimulates an inhibitory effect on somatic pain perception."

Whatever way you choose to stimulate your vagus nerve to create a positive balance, you are putting your body's chemistry in a pro-healing, anti-inflammatory state. Once you have achieved changes using these techniques, they should become a part of your daily routine. This ability is a part of your being. Embrace it. Step into your power. You are transitioning from the darkness into the light.

Meditation and washing your face with ice cold water are other ways of naturally stimulating your vagus nerve. Most people think of meditation as boring or something that requires practice. In the companion guide, I explain how to use self-hypnosis to create the same mentally relaxed state experienced in meditation. With practice, you can do it quickly and easily to immerse yourself in love, gratitude, and comfort.

The next time I saw Gwen, she was ecstatic. She went through her 4-hour surgery with no nausea, very little pain, and only received one dose of pain medication after surgery through the IV. She said when waking up in recovery that she didn't even feel like she had anesthesia! She had been admitted overnight because the doctor expected her to need pain control through the IV. Gwen was blown away and did not understand why all patients aren't given this option when they go in for surgery.

Let me recap this last point because it's so important: we can naturally trigger our body to halt stress activation and inflammation. This interruption is immediate. What's more, with consistency we can shift the chemical balance throughout our body, promoting expression of healing genes. Here's what I suggest you do next: pick at least one way you can naturally stimulate your vagus nerve and use it. So go ahead and get started right now, because it's free and you have complete control of it!

Move Forward!

What will you do this week to bring balance back?

Sing a favorite song

Meditate

Breathe

Laugh at a funny video or joke

Pick one and set aside 5 minutes each day to do it. Then head on over to https://facebook.com/groups/thefibrocode and share what you did today!

"As a single footstep will not make a path on the earth, so a single thought will not make a pathway in the mind. To make a deep physical path, we walk again and again. To make a deep mental path, we must think over and over the kind of thoughts we wish to dominate our lives."

Wilfred Arlan Peterson

CHAPTER 3

Breaking the Cycle

"You are not your thoughts. You are the thinker of your thoughts."

Jim Fortin

Feeling a loss of control is a common problem for those diagnosed with fibromyalgia and other chronic pain syndromes. Fortunately, however, fibro conquerers don't have to suffer from helplessness and hopelessness once they know how to begin taking control over their physiology.

That's what you'll learn about in this chapter. Specifically, you'll learn how to begin moving your attention and why that's important. You'll also learn about what mindfulness is and how it can help you. And you'll even discover how to take a proper breath and its influence over body chemistry. So, without delay, let's jump in with a discussion of how thoughts can make you sick.

Marla had had enough. For 20 years, she had been taking medication to help her relax and to sleep. She woke up groggy and didn't want to do this anymore. A very shy woman in her 60s, she slowly began to open up. Years earlier, after caring for her ailing mother up until her passing, she began to have this issue. Every night when she lay down, she could not stop the thoughts running through her head. Even now, if she did not take the relaxation medication before the sleep medication, the worrying thoughts returned when she lay down at night.

Thoughts can become habit

Our subconscious mind operates on loops. We have a thought, and the mind assigns meaning to it. We experience feelings, and a behavior follows. This is how our mind forms patterns for beliefs and habits. Even when we are unaware, the subconscious mind is taking in data, processing it and accepting it, or rejecting it based on our network of beliefs.

> *Stress is a part of life. Even our thoughts can cause stress and make the body susceptible to illness.*[10]

Sometimes when we have a thought, a flood of others follows it. If we do not know the answer or have enough information to make sense of the thought, our mind will generate a new one or a question. This happens to everyone once in a while, if we are not aware of our thinking. Depending on where your mind is, the first thought might occur, and you immediately notice it is absurd and shut down your thinking. Or, you may end up down the rabbit hole of the mind, in a spiral of negative thinking.

> *"Attention on physical symptoms [thinking] results in an increased intensity of symptoms…"*[11]

Our subconscious mind forms habits without conscious awareness. If we go down the rabbit hole of the mind often, runaway thinking can become an unconscious habit. Now keep in mind every thought generates a chemical response in the brain, even subconscious thoughts.

Now in a positive light, children daydream and get lost in thought all the time. They have a positive idea, then begin to imagine themselves there and off they go. As adults, we tend to have a negative thought, and that turns into worry. When we unconsciously immerse ourselves into the feelings of a negative thought, we actually begin to enter a light hypnotic state and begin to program our minds for negativity. This begins to rewire the brain through a process called neuroplasticity.

For Marla, she was always busy during the day caring for her mother. When she got quiet at night, the thoughts would come. Over time, her mind made the connection that when she lay down at night, she paid attention to her thoughts. A disruptive, unhealthy brain-based habit was born. In order to interrupt this pattern, I introduced her to a couple of techniques she could use.

You are where your attention is

In the last chapter, I suggested that you begin to become aware of your thoughts and where they are taking you. Every day, most of us (me included) go through a good part of the day mindlessly. What do I mean by mindlessly? We are engaged in our routines, doing things based on habit, without giving thought to what we are doing.

When we give thought to what we are doing, our attention is on what we are doing rather than going through the motions while our subconscious runs amuck in an emotional playground. The best example I have of this is driving. Once you've been driving for a while, it is a habit. You don't have to think about stopping for a stop sign. You just do it. Driving is one of the most common times we get lost in thought. Let me give you an example of how this act can make or break your day.

It's early in the morning, and you woke up five minutes late. As you are moving around the house getting ready to go into work, you make up the gap. Then as you walk out the door to the car, you spill coffee on your shirt. You hurry back inside, change your shirt, then head back out the door and hop into the car. Once in the vehicle, your day can go one of two ways. Maybe you think to yourself, "Well, that was great. At least

I don't have a meeting, so five minutes won't matter." Or maybe you start beating up yourself with, "Dammit, I am going to be late again. Watch. I'll catch every red light. At noon, I have to meet with John, and that's just great. He never agrees with anything I have to say. I swear I hate this job. Why can't I just get out?"

"Negative emotion influences [pain] sensitization and may increase functional disability."[12]

With the second example of driving along, you enter a light trance, which begins to program your mind very negatively. The theme of the entire thought process is that you're not good enough. The emotions are fear, anger, sadness, frustration, even hate. Wow! Imagine what those negative emotions are doing to the body.

When you find yourself having negative thoughts, say to yourself, "Stop it!" and move your attention somewhere else. Sometimes your subconscious isn't going to like this. Especially when this has become an unconscious habit. You must repeat this process over and over. Your subconscious mind will even generate thoughts like "you can't do this" or "this is stupid." That is because the subconscious is protecting the status quo. It finds safety in the status quo, even if it is hurting you. Be persistent, and you will break the neural connections. You will be amazed at how quickly you become aware of your mind trying to run away with you in the future. You will be amazing.

"Mentally trying to solve the problem of pain, and prevent negative consequences of results in stronger pain due to neural processing bias [brain signal processing]."[13]

Master your thoughts and master your life

It is not enough to stop negative thinking. We want to begin to shift to thoughts that serve us in a positive way. This is a hot button for you.

I know it, and right now, I am rolling my eyes so I can let go of what I hear you screaming in my ears. This is important! Yes, you are tired of hearing people telling you to think positive. If you need to throw the book and cuss me out again, go ahead. I'll be here when you get back. I'm not talking about wishful thinking, unicorns, and rainbows. When thoughts are negative, pain is amplified. By shifting to positive, you avoid this amplification. It is one more piece in the puzzle of your code.

When you experience negative thoughts, like the ones above, turn it around. For example, take:

"At noon I have to meet with John, and that's just great. He never agrees with anything I have to say."

and turn it around:

"So what if I have to meet with John. My ideas are good even if he doesn't like them."

or

"John may not like my ideas, but I put a lot of effort into them. What he thinks does not affect my happiness."

If you start hitting all the red lights and you're late, observe that it's possible that the red light has helped you avoid being involved in an accident. That there is a reason the universe is slowing you down today. Everything is about how you frame it.

"Conscious thought has powerful influence on the fear center [amygdala] and can stop fear activation."[14]

Another way to master your thoughts is to practice mindfulness. When I first heard about mindfulness, I was like, "Yeah, whatever." That is until I started to understand it and use it. Now, I know it works. When your attention is on what you are doing, your subconscious "monkey" mind isn't chattering away and jumping down negative rabbit holes. Your attention is in the present moment and not the past or a future we cannot predict. When your attention is on the task at hand, the very task becomes a form of mindfulness meditation.

"In a recent review, Black and Slavich (2016), suggest that mindfulness meditation appears to be associated with decreases in pro-inflammatory actions and increases an enzyme that prevents cell aging."

Let's look at a task you dislike. For example (from my real life), I do not have a dishwasher. I choose to be the primary financial provider, and my husband enjoys working on an "as needed basis" for his projects. Many days, I come home to find the sink overflowing with dishes. In the past, I got upset. Downright triggered. Once I started practicing mindfulness, I recognized two things. One, I stay in my power and internal peace if I just do the dishes and two, I am grateful that I have dishes, food to eat off of them, and hot water to clean them.

My attention is on this gratitude when I clean my husband's breakfast and lunch dishes. It does not stress me because I do not allow it.

What is one area in your life that you can choose to no longer give up your power and have internal peace? A small research study out of Stamford demonstrated that gratitude can lessen the severity of depression and anxiety. Look for opportunities to be grateful in everything you do.

Using the breath as a mindfulness technique

Marla used the "relaxing breath." a.k.a. diaphragmatic breathing as a mindfulness technique. When Marla learned the breath, for the first week she used it 3-4 breaths, once per hour during the day, and then when she lay down to go to sleep at night. After that first week, she used it whenever she needed to during the day if she was having worrying thoughts and at bedtime. By focusing attention on proper breathing, the mind cannot focus on worry. Throughout the rest of the book, I will refer to proper abdominal breath as the relaxing breath.

When learning to take a proper relaxing breath, you want to be sitting or standing. Relax your shoulders. Loosen them up if you need to. Now imagine that you have an empty balloon in your stomach. We want to inflate that balloon, but unlike a balloon that you blow up with your mouth, you blow this balloon up when you inhale. Take a breath in and let it all the way out. Now take in a very big breath, allowing your lungs to push your diaphragm down into your belly 1, 2, 3. Hold it 1, 2, 3. Now let it out 1, 2, 3, 4, 5, 6.

When you took this deep breath, if you pushed your chest up and out and your shoulders back, you pulled the air into your upper chest. Try it again, but this time do it differently. You want your chest and shoulders relaxed, with the diaphragm moving down into your stomach as the lungs expand. As you practice, focus on the feeling of the air going into your lungs, and the relaxation of your muscles as the air flows out. The lung expansion stretches your vagus nerve and the pressure increases in your abdomen during this full breath. Not only does the breath move your attention, but it also activates the vitality response in your body.

"Diaphragmatic breathing resulting in changes that lowered free radicals and oxidative stress."[15]

When I last saw Marla, she was amazed at how a systematic process of releasing old emotion, along with learning two simple techniques to stop thoughts in their tracks, changed her life. Marla was excited to be working with her doctor to safely taper off medications she had been taking for 20 years. Marla learned that the "why" did not matter; it was about how to step back into her power.

You just discovered how you can move your attention and use mindfulness techniques to become more comfortable and focused by decreasing activation of the automated stress response. However, a word of warning – just knowing how to do a diaphragmatic breath and move your attention isn't going to create a chemical state that supports healing. That's because the key is that you need to take action on what you just learned. I encourage you to review chapter 2, review the connection to your health, and then start implementing the breath and shifting your attention right away. Because the sooner you do, the sooner you'll feel in control of your health and your life!

Visit www.thefibrocode.com/resources to get access to a free video teaching you a powerful technique for using the breath to halt inflammation!

"The closer you come to knowing that you alone create the world of your experience, the more vital it becomes for you to discover just who is doing the creating."

Eric Micha'el Leventhal

CHAPTER 4

Design your Destiny

*"The mind has great influence over the body and
maladies often have their origin there."*

Moliére 1622-1673

Seeing a way beyond where you are is a challenge when you suffer from fibromyalgia and chronic pain. Fibro conquerers don't have to suffer from endless pain once they know how to reprogram the mind for comfort. That's what you'll learn about in this chapter. Specifically, you'll learn how the brain creates chronic pain through neuroplasticity. You'll also find out how hypnosis takes advantage of neuroplasticity to create new neural pathways. And you'll even discover how you can begin to explore hypnosis to create more comfort in your life. So, without further introduction, let's jump in with a discussion of how the mind develops beliefs and patterns in your life.

Almost 100 percent of us live in our past. Every decision we make is based on our experience. Our experience comes from past events.

These past events have shaped our emotional responses and beliefs within the subconscious mind. The patterns of our lives are rooted in the subconscious belief system we have.

To objectively observe and recognize when we are living in the past, we need to understand how our mind processes information. Once we can identify the patterns, we can move beyond old beliefs that no longer serve us. Then we can take our ability to master our thoughts to the next level.

Feelings are emotions in disguise

When we are born, our subconscious mind is blank. Our brain records all events and the importance of those events by placing meaning and emotion on them. Now you may be thinking you cannot recall any memories before age 3 or 4. The mind may not have an explicit memory, but it has impressions of love, sadness, safety, fear, anger, etc. The familiarity of a feeling is far more powerful than the memory itself. Emotions in the subconscious mind generate our physical feelings.

As I learned from my mentor, Cal Banyan, it is easiest to compare the subconscious mind to the rings of a tree. The center ring represents the small sapling. Each year, a ring of wood is added as the tree weathers the elements. Each year, the tree gets bigger, and the bark becomes tougher and thicker. The same thing happens with our experiences. They do not disappear. They are always there, easily accessible to the subconscious.

As we grow from babies and have experiences in life, the SCM takes that information and begins to interpret it.

When something happens, we consciously and subconsciously place meaning on it. Once the subconscious has identified or placed meaning upon the event, it generates an emotion. The emotion activates areas in the brain that stimulate the ASR or vitality response, resulting in feelings. The way we feel drives our behavior. Once we have engaged in a behavior, our subconscious notes how that makes us feel. Then we await the next something to happen.

You can create a new reality

Over time, our SCM identifies patterns. Either our needs are met, or they are not. We feel safe and secure, or we do not. We feel sad and unloved, or loved and cared for. We are hungry, or we are satisfied. We feel we are enough, or we do not. Every event we experience begins to add to our memories and generate patterns. Out of those patterns arise our beliefs about ourselves, our environment, and the world around us.

The unconscious mind is the operating system of the body, generating our vital signs and activating habits associated with survival. The subconscious mind is made up of the programs we run. These programs can be helpful or hurtful, and they are 100% based in the past.

Most of the time, when we have less than helpful programming, we can make small adjustments and overcome it. For some people, events occur in life that resonates with those old emotions. In other words, the situation generates a feeling that is so similar to an earlier feeling that the subconscious ties those events together. Then another event occurs.

The mind continues to connect these dots until one day, you suddenly find yourself having an anxiety attack over something you have done hundreds of times with no problem. Where did this come from? When you experienced that event, the subconscious mind responded with the intensity of all of those past events. The SCM is generating exaggerated fear because it is sensing danger from the past and present.

Sometimes the SCM will generate physical pain in an attempt to get our attention. We can't make sense of it, because how are we supposed to know the sensation and experience of pain caused by emotional injury? Usually, anger and frustration will generate stress and tension within the muscles. Myofascial pain syndrome has long been identified as one of many pain disorders associated with emotional pain. Fibromyalgia also has a strong association with emotional events in childhood or trauma.

In the same way that you can delete, update, or replace programs on your computer, you can do the same in the subconscious. You cannot delete memories, but you can remove old, inaccurate feelings and inter-pretations around events. You can replace programs that no longer serve you through the repetition of new thoughts and actions. When the subconscious mind realizes you are bypassing those erroneous reactions by reprogramming yourself, it adopts a new way of thinking.

"Hypnosis, meditation, and Pavlovian conditioning can modulate inflammation through vagal mechanisms."[16]

The first step in reprogramming your mind is *deciding what you want.* It is tempting to focus on one small thing. But what is your purpose for reading this book? Who do you want to be? Once you know what you want, you can identify the beliefs you need to have to be that person. When you know the beliefs you must have to achieve that; you know what steps you need to take. Now that you know the steps you need to take, you can begin to reprogram your mind.

Using repetition and pushing through your comfort zone is one way of reprogramming your mind. It takes consistent repetition, and you have to be sure to avoid using will power. Will power is a conscious function and is limited in its ability to assist in change. Will power is similar to a cell phone battery. After a full day of use, when you need it the most, the battery runs down. With will power, you enter an internal argument with your SCM, and in the end, the SCM will win.

The fastest and easiest way to reprogram your SCM is by using hypnosis. Hypnosis is safe and effective in reprogramming new beliefs. Hypnosis has been recognized as a phenomenon for creating change for over two centuries. Franz Anton Mesmer, the father of hypnosis, used what he called the "theory of animal magnetism" to help others heal.

In the 1800s, James Esdaile, a physician and surgeon, learned mesmerism and adapted the technique to induce trance and render his patients completely insensitive to pain. His records show he performed over 1,000 minor and 250 major operations painlessly. In the 1950s, Dave Elman, a stage hypnotist, was conducting a charity event when his skill was recognized by a physician. Shortly after, Mr. Elman began to teach hypnosis exclusively to physicians and dentists.

Hypnosis is associated with the same brain wave frequencies as deep meditation. Deep meditation is associated with epigenetic changes influencing healing.[171819]

Helping people eliminate pain is my passion

I have been in the nursing profession since 1994, and an anesthetist since 2005. I was in local hospitals or larger teaching facilities. It always intrigued me how someone's state of mind influenced how well they progressed through treatments or surgery. Just two years into my nursing career, I remember saying things to patients like, "You have a great attitude, and that is half the battle."

To demonstrate the opposite, I'll never forget a patient who had convinced himself his surgery was the most painful. No matter what anyone did, he was going to wake up in excruciating pain. I knew the anesthetic we were giving. I know anatomy and physiology. When he awoke from sedation, I know he was numb from his waist down by assessment. Yet, he screamed and cried out hysterically in pain because he had created the expectation of pain in his mind, and that was exactly what was going to happen.

In 2008, while creating a continuing education course on pain for a local nursing presentation, I stumbled across the scientific data supporting hypnosis. It made me curious. In 2013, I became certified in hypnosis by another nurse anesthetist. I wanted someone who could connect the scientific dots for me.

When I entered that course, I never intended to become a practicing hypnotist. What I experienced in that course removed any doubts I had about the power of the mind to create comfort and heal. This is when I decided to set out on a path to help others release their pain.

The effectiveness of hypnosis in pain management and many other diseases is well documented. If it is a disease that goes hand in hand with activation of the stress response, hypnosis can help. 70-90% of doctor's visits and 50% of all missed work days are for symptoms related to stress.

"...hypnotic strategies are equivalent or more effective than other treatments for both acute and chronic pain, and they are likely to save both money and time for patients and clinicians."

Drs. Patterson and Jensen

All hypnosis is self-hypnosis

Hypnosis is simply a state of focused attention. When the attention is focused, the conscious analytical mind is not actively engaged. In this state, the subconscious can be provided with suggestions or insights for change. So many people say they don't believe they can be hypnotized, yet they have spaced out while driving, or even caught themselves daydreaming. It is the same state of mind. To be guided into hypnosis, either by audio or in person, you need to be able to follow instructions. Period.

Sometimes people will ask me what is the difference between hypnosis and meditation or guided visualization. It is the intent of the practice. They are all the same state of mind. The conscious mind goes quiet, allowing the subconscious to receive suggestions. This decreases internal stress inputs in the brain and allows the vitality response to dominate the physiology. The practitioner enters the state with a different intention.

All hypnosis is self-hypnosis. This includes stage hypnosis. The client has to want to be hypnotized for a hypnotist to guide a client into that state. They also have to feel comfortable and safe on a subconscious level. If there is any fear, it can interfere with the process. Now you might be thinking, "But stage hypnotists make those people do crazy things!" No, they don't. The volunteers know it's going to be a fun and crazy time, and the very nature of volunteering gives consent subconsciously to the process. Even if you are doing self-hypnosis at home, and someone were to knock on the door, you would be aware.

Hypnosis is associated with decreased stress response activity reducing inflammatory reactions in the skin and pain sensitivity.[20]

Your mind is a very powerful tool. It is at your disposal, anytime and anywhere. It doesn't cost you anything to use it. This powerful tool can be used for good or bad. If you sit and worry and your mind starts envisioning all of the things that can go wrong, you are sending signals into the brain to 1) search for the negatives around you and 2) that you fear for your sense of well-being and safety. When the brain is primed for pessimism, your stress response is activated. Worry is negative self-hypnosis.

I am not saying to ignore threats. Be aware of your circumstances and responsibility and focus on what you have in the moment. Even if things are not going well in life, you can program your mind to seek out the positive, the silver lining. You can program your mind to create an expectation of feeling better every day. Over time, it will notice the discomfort less and less.

"…75% of clinical and experimental participants with different types of pain obtained substantial pain relief from hypnotic techniques."[21]

Guy Montgomery, PhD, Katherine DuHamel, PhD, and William Redd, PhD

Neuroplasticity and the changes that take place in the brain to create chronic pain is the brain learning a new way to be. To reverse this, we have to relearn how to be comfortable and to have an expectation of feeling good, instead of waiting for the other shoe to drop. Living in constant subconscious fear is destroying your life.

You can begin right now. Close your eyes. Take five or six of your diaphragmatic breaths and feel yourself start to relax as you breathe out any tension in your body. Imagine waking up in the morning comfortable. Say to yourself, "I feel better today," while smiling and loving your comfortable body. Then get out of bed refreshed and ready to face your day. The beauty of this process is that you can use whatever image you desire. Feel the emotion that goes with that picture of health, comfort, and peace.

Many people with chronic pain have a lot of emotions entangled in the pain experience. It can be from past events or anger and sadness over life in pain. Private sessions with an experienced hypnotist who understands chronic pain can help you identify and release these emotions. Hypnotist-led sessions can help you achieve change faster than self-hypnosis alone. In Chapters 9 and 10, you will read about two women who experienced radical improvement in their lives, releasing discomfort using hypnosis.

Let me reiterate the key point, simply because it's so important: you can use hypnosis to take advantage of the same mechanism that wired your brain for chronic pain to create comfort. What's more, hypnosis is a proven, effective way to eliminate or change the sensations you feel and engage your vitality response. Here's what I suggest you do next: decide how you want to feel and write down what your day looks like, how it feels to be more comfortable. Then use the technique I described above to begin training your mind to go quiet and focus on your outcome. Go ahead and get started right now, because it takes repetition to get your mind used to this new way of being!

Move Forward!

Take as long as you like and sit down and write out what your day looks like when you are completely comfortable. Write out all of the positive feelings and thoughts that go with that. Share your vision with the community at https://facebook.com/groups/thefibrocode, then use the above technique three times a day to reprogram your mind.

"Words are singularly the most powerful force available to humanity. We can choose to use this force constructively with words of encouragement, or destructively using words of despair. Words have energy and power with the ability to help, to heal, to hinder, to hurt, to harm, to humiliate, and to humble."

Dr. Zahed

CHAPTER 5

The Power of Words

"Learning to negotiate thoughtless, careless, or uninformed statements from family friends and doctors enhances morale."

David Spiegel, Living Beyond Limits

There's an old adage, "The pen is mightier than the sword." What exactly does that mean? It goes to the heart of this chapter, and that is the power of words. Maybe you've always understood that words and language can influence people, even hurt people. It goes even much deeper than that. In this chapter, I will show you the importance of the how and the why so that you can become aware and protect your health at all levels.

Who is suggestible?

In the previous chapter, we talked about hypnosis and how it is a heightened state of suggestibility. However suggestibility can exist in the absence of a hypnotic trance. Suggestibility is believed at some level to be an inborn trait in us as humans. There are certain circumstances believed to influence suggestibility, and it has more to do with the way that the mind is functioning at the time than any predisposition.

Take, for example, people who work in a monotonous job, such as a worker on an assembly line at an auto plant. Individuals keep performing the same actions over and over without engaging the critical aspect of the mind to perform the task. These individuals have unknowingly developed a level of conditioning where they are mindlessly performing the task. In this state, the individual is more suggestible to outside statements and influence. It is believed that this suggestibility carries over into other areas of their life.

Another example of an individual who might be more suggestible is a soldier who is accustomed to performing according to orders. When young soldiers go through training, they are conditioned to not question their orders. Under stress, they need to be able to carry out essential functions without thinking about them. This level of conditioning may or may not carry over into other areas of their life.

Not only do we have a baseline level of suggestibility, but there are everyday experiences that bring us in and out of trance moments to increase our suggestibility. We've already talked about worry being a form of negative self-hypnosis. A state of worry is a trance moment.

Natural light trance

Trance moments can occur when we are in a relaxed setting having a casual conversation or engaged in intense activity. When we're in a light trance moment, we can be startled easily. For example, have you ever been working at something—either a hobby or balancing a checkbook—something that has your mind engaged? Then someone walked up beside you and startled you?

Something very similar could happen while taking a walk down the street. You're listening to music in your headphones, oblivious to what's going on around you. You walk past the neighbor's yard. This neighbor has a dog who likes you and has never hurt you. He loves to charge out of the backyard to the front yard barking aggressively. It's his favorite pastime. It may be that you like this dog, but in this particular moment, because your conscious mind is passive and you're in a light trance state, the startled response and the emotion of fear imprints itself into your subconscious. You're more highly suggestible in this state. Now, you've developed an unease and avoid walking on that side of the street near that dog, even though you know he won't hurt you. Your subconscious mind has now associated that dog and that yard with the fear response.

Healthy skepticism is a good thing

It is ever important to be mindful of your attention. It's easy to see people talk about mindfulness on YouTube, Facebook, and TV shows. Did you ever wonder to yourself, "What a bunch of woo-woo is this?" It would be most helpful if people would take the time to explain the point of mindfulness and why it is so important to practice it. Mindfulness is not a five-minute exercise that you do each day and discard it. It needs to become the way that you live. Mindfulness means your conscious awareness is engaged in whatever it is that you are doing. When we practice mindfulness, the subconscious mind is not engaged in wild thoughts, running amok. When we practice mindfulness, we are using our comparing mechanism in evaluating the information that we are receiving.

This healthy skepticism is an absolute must any time that you're on social media, watching TV, or viewing commercials. All of these media are created to influence you. They influence your purchasing decisions, your overall sense of well-being (stress response, anyone?), and even your beliefs about your health. So what does all of this have to do with chronic pain and your health? Hang on; I'm getting there!

Authenticity and trust increase suggestibility

There are two other situations that increase your suggestibility. This is of particular interest to you as someone diagnosed with chronic pain. People are generally more suggestible when receiving information from people in a position of authority, including doctors, nurses, physical therapists, and other healthcare providers. Not only did they carry a degree of authority, but there is a huge degree of trust because we generally avoid putting our health and well-being into the hands of people that we do not trust. I am about to show you how their words can literally affect your health.

The power of the mind to heal

I want to introduce to you the placebo effect. The placebo effect refers to a non-therapeutic treatment given to patients. They receive a benefit from it because they expect or believe that it will work. It does not only work with non-therapeutic treatments. Even with known effective treatments the benefits are enhanced by belief. Emile Coué, a French psychologist and pharmacist, wrote of enhanced benefits and healing when positive suggestions were given with medications. He wrote of the power of autosuggestion, a phenomenon dating back to the time of Aristotle. Coué is most famously known for his healing statement, "Day by day, in every way, I am getting better and better."

> *"Placebo can occur when morale is high…the conditions for healing are enhanced."*[22]

If the right words with a placebo can effect a cure, imagine what the right words with effective treatment can do!

The placebo effect is associated with *real physiological and neurochemical changes.* Some speculate it is merely the belief that healing is going to occur. It relaxes the tension within the stress response system allowing the natural healing of the body to take place. The exact mechanism remains unknown. In a recent study out of Blackpool, England, with over one hundred participants, part of the group acted as a control, with the rest being told they would be included in the study, receiving either the placebo or a powerful new painkiller. However, they all received placeboes. The pills were dressed up to look like real pharmaceutical bottles labeled with warnings of side effects.

More than half of all participants had significant relief from taking these pills. Another major difference in this study is that half of the participants received little more than nine minutes of time with the physician to discuss their back pain before being given the pills and shown out of the office. The other group had double that amount of time. The amount of time spent with the doctor had a huge effect on the outcome. Those who had more time with the physician had greater benefit. This goes back to reinforce Coué's observations that suggestion, along with treatment, yielded greater results.

"When motivation, caring, and trust come together in balance, we get placebo. Out of balance we get nocebo."[23]

Unfortunately, the opposite can also occur. This effect is called the nocebo effect. This was originally demonstrated when study participants experienced negative reactions to a dummy drug that was given based on the belief and expectation that it was a harmful and dangerous drug.

This is not the only circumstance where the nocebo effect can take place. If you happen to be in any online pain communities, how often have you read a post that says, "Do you experience_____ with fibromyalgia?" Then you scroll, and you read the responses. Maybe you don't have this symptom, but the more you read about it, you start to think, "You know what? I have felt this before." Your subconscious starts to pay attention. Unconsciously, you begin looking for it. The next thing you know, you have developed this symptom, too.

Maybe you are like some women diagnosed with fibromyalgia, and your doctor says something like, "You have fibromyalgia. You can expect to be diagnosed with lupus within a year, and you'll probably die of MS." This is an actual comment, made to a woman at a doctor's visit. As a healthcare professional with experience of how the mind works, this shocks me. The nocebo effect is well documented, and this is one of the many reasons I am passionate about getting this information to you. There is nothing wrong with asking your doctor to not suggest symptoms or illness to you that you are not experiencing unless your diagnostics tests show actual cause for concern or diagnosis.

Are your doctor's words harming you

One of the most important aspects of treatment or therapy is the way in which it is presented to the person receiving it. Doctors are truly well-meaning. If a doctor gives you medication and says, "I don't know if this will work, but maybe it will help. We'll try it and see. If it doesn't, we'll move on to something else," he or she has created a possible expectation of likely failure. If you have a pattern of moving through treatments that have not worked and have become skeptical that a treatment will help, your subconscious is in a position to be influenced negatively by those statements.

Because you are reading this book, I already know that you know treatments don't achieve the same results for everyone. Approach your options with optimism. Ask your doctor when he/she is making changes to prescriptions or treatments to explain the positive aspects of what they are doing. Concentrate on those points as you start treatment.

I also wonder if you've ever noticed that any time you need to have a medical procedure done or start a new medication, people come out of the woodwork to tell you their horrible experiences. They can create an expectation in you that is extremely negative. It could be that this treatment or this medication is exactly what you need. Now you've been given an expectation that it will not work.

Fortunately, you are not powerless to the words of the people around you. It is why I emphasize being mindful of where your attention is. If you're fully absorbed in conversation with your friends, your physician, your nurse, or other healthcare providers, you may unknowingly accept these statements as absolute truth in the subconscious mind. When you sit in that doctor's office, listen with an air of healthy skepticism.

Self-talk can be your most dangerous enemy, or your greatest ally

Not only are the words of trusted friends and people in authority influential, but your own words play a role. If treatments in the past have not worked as well as you would've liked and you've convinced yourself that nothing is ever going to work, that you have no hope, and there is no cure—then you are exactly right. From Emile Coue's My Method to the present-day research on chronic pain by Mark Jansen and others, it is crystal clear. The way you view your situation and talk about it is a known predictor of the success of your treatment according to pain research out of Stamford and other universities. How you talk to yourself matters. Your words influence your subconscious belief. The benefit of your belief aligning with the treatment that you are receiving is profound.

You just discovered how powerful words are to your state of health. However, a word of warning – that doesn't mean your healthcare providers and close friends are aware of this power. *That's why you need to take action on what you just learned.* I encourage you to educate your healthcare providers, friends, and family on how their words impact your health and then join my Facebook group, Breaking the Fibro Code, to join a community of people living beyond their chronic pain, who are very aware of the power of words. The sooner you do, the sooner you'll feel connected with others seeking to reclaim their life!

Move Forward!

Make a note of friends or doctors with whom you would like to share this new knowledge. You can take this book with you to the doctor to share, or go to www.thefibrocode.com/resources and get a free download to share with your healthcare providers.

"Everything is within your power,

and your power is within you."

***Janice Trachtman, Catching What Life Throws at You:
Inspiring True Stories of Healing***

CHAPTER 6

Claim Your POWER

"You are in 100% influence of the circumstances of your life."

Jim Fortin

The ultimate goal is to shift your subconscious so that it is working for you, and for what you want. This means you have to take a look at the world around you and your relationship with it. It is something fibro conquerors deal with all the time. You may sometimes find yourself living your life in the shadow of your diagnosis, but that is not the only area of your life where this comes into play. How you see yourself and your place in the game of life defines your life.

This applies to every being on the planet. No one is immune from what I am about to share with you. The key is becoming aware of this way of thinking, and if you realize you think this way some times, stop yourself. If this way of thinking has become a habit, you must stop it to feel better. When you have chronic pain, and you think this way consistently, you will experience greater depression, greater anxiety, and poor pain relief. You are the only one with the power to stop it.

Each day life goes on. It does not matter if you are sick or healthy. Rich or poor. The sun rises and sets, and you live in a world where you cannot push pause and wait until you feel better to push play. We are sharing the planet with 7 billion other people, and like you, they are busy living their lives as well.

Everyone is in their own world

They are busy making their own choices. While the things they do may affect events in your life, they are not doing it to you. It is easy to say something like, "That jerk cut me off! I could have wrecked my car." When you say something like this, you make the situation about you. It creates a subconscious perception of unfair, which activates your stress response, which is unnecessary because this had nothing to do with you.

When you have an experience like someone cutting you off, the most powerful place to work from is one of compassion and gratitude. By experiencing gratitude that you were attentive and safe, you can take a moment to feel compassion because:

Maybe he is just an angry person, and that's no way to live.
Maybe he was distracted and did not see you.
Every car has a blind spot.
Maybe he has inflammatory bowel disease and needs a toilet now!
Maybe his child is sick, and he is rushing to be by their side.

The bottom line is that for whatever reason, he did what he did, but it is not about you. It is a choice to make it personal. You can choose to operate from a place of power or react negatively.

Most of the time, it's not the jerk cutting you off that is the problem. It is the people or situations you find yourselves in almost every day. Perhaps you have an overly critical boss. Every day you go in and never seem to have a good day. When you try to make things better, the problem becomes worse. This is because you are focused on the problem, not the solution. You may be asking questions like "Why does _____ always have to say something bad about my work?" The quality of our lives depends upon the quality of questions we ask. How will knowing "why" change anything? It doesn't. It only serves to make you feel bad, which perpetuates the vicious cycle of allowing your thoughts, and as a result, your feelings to control you.

"A problem cannot be solved from the same level of thinking that created it"

~Albert Einstein.

Asking yourself the right questions elevates you above the problem

By asking the right questions, you are reclaiming your power. The power enables you with the ability to choose how to respond and whether or not you will allow someone or some situation to make you feel. Defining your life in the context of circumstances makes you powerless. You are not powerless. You have the power of choice. The one thing you came into this world with that no one can take from you is the ability to choose. You can choose to exist as a result of others' actions or be responsible for how you feel and respond. Often, you won't like your choices. As a result, you might do nothing. Doing nothing is also a choice.

Once you arrive at a place of knowing everything is choice, you begin to realize you are the writer of your life's book. This unveils the power that you have within you. I understand. You did not ask for the situation you were born into. You did not ask for chronic discomfort and disease. I agree 100%. We have power through choice. Embrace this, and it will shift your entire way of being. On the darkest day, knowing you decided to do or be who you need to be in that moment takes away any hold fibromyalgia once held over you. Stay with me, and I will show you how choice and the right strategies can empower you to live your best life.

In the following examples, it is not my intention, nor is it possible to address all of the potential factors.

Example 1.

It is raining outside, and your pain has been on the increase. Today, it is just too much. There is a load of laundry that needs washing. It hurts so bad you cannot even think of doing it. It hurts to move. It is an "I just can't get out of bed" kind of day. Never mind everything else that needs doing.

Fibromyalgia didn't kick your butt into staying in bed all day. You were having a bad day with fibro, and you chose to stay in bed. Maybe that's exactly what your body needed. That's okay. It was your choice.

Example 2.

The last week or so, you weren't your best, but you kept pushing through. You woke up feeling great. You are energetic and focused. There is a to-do list that grew over the last two weeks because you conserved energy so you could work. Today is the day to go all in. Even though you know overworking muscles that you haven't used recently is going to make you sore, and you will hurt so severely tomorrow that you can't move. It did not all have to be done today, but you chose to do it.

Example 3.

You have been recently diagnosed with fibromyalgia. The doctor gave you some medication. He said it might work, but most likely, you'll have to live with the pain. Not only will it get worse, but there is no treatment. You have several choices here. You can take the doctor at his word and go through life waiting for the other shoe to drop. You can do nothing. You can get a second opinion, or you can seek out information on things you can do to maintain control of your life.

You always have a choice

Let's take this one step further. When you go into support groups, almost everyone reinforces there is no hope or cure. Then you see one person who says they did what *everyone else says doesn't work*, and they have reversed their symptoms and are back in the game of life. Those who believe they are stuck in this place with no hope attack this person and say they didn't really have fibromyalgia. You can join in this way of thinking, or you can choose to be curious and open to the possibility. Which gives you more power?

It is never hopeless. You are never out of options. You are never at the mercy of a diagnosis. A powerful place to work from is to be someone diagnosed with fibromyalgia rather than owning the disease — "I have fibromyalgia." Long before I understood how language and thoughts impact our mind and our health, my husband was diagnosed with multiple sclerosis. That was over 20 years ago. He would reject any attempt to design our lives around the diagnosis beyond my returning to school to further my degree. I don't believe I have ever heard him say, "I have MS." He separates his life so far from that diagnosis that, at times, I forget he was even diagnosed. I have to catch myself if he is having a restless, fatigue-filled day. It is my belief that he is now the fittest and healthiest he has ever been because of his powerful attitude toward the diagnosis.

Always remember the one thing we came into this world with is the power to choose. We often may not like our choices and as a result, do nothing. Doing nothing is a choice. If you find yourself saying, "This doesn't apply to me because of x, y, or z," you are living your life in reaction to external events. You have given over the power of choice to respond to your circumstances.

Every day I see fibro conquerors taking back their power by choosing to make changes in the way they think, believe, and act to be healthier. When you experience loss of control, then pain, depression, and related issues can worsen. Look at your environment and assume control of the things you have power over. Take control of the way you allow circumstances to make you feel. A sense of control leads to improved outcomes in pain and related issues. This is not about denial. It is about acknowledging your diagnosis or situation and choosing to not allow it to control you.

You just discovered how the way you view situations in your life can negatively influence your subconscious thinking. However, a word of caution – just knowing how important it is to stop this way of thinking and view your life in the world isn't going to eliminate how it impacts the way you feel. That's because the key is that you need to take action on what you just learned. That's why I encourage you to become aware of the statements you make and thoughts you have that define your life. When you find you are doing it, tell yourself to stop! Then reframe the statement from a place of power. Implement this strategy right away because the sooner you do, the sooner you'll start to increase your comfort and the joy and optimism you experience in life.

Move Forward!

What is a common situation you find yourself in where you can shift your perspective to one that empowers you through choice? Having a difficult time finding a way to shift the perspective? Ask the community of fibro conquerors in Breaking the Fibro Code Facebook group for their advice at https://facebook.com/groups/TheFibroCode.

"*They caused the first wound, but you are causing the rest; this is what not forgiving does. They got it started, but you keep it going. Forgive and let it go, or it will eat you alive. You think they made you feel this way, but when you won't forgive, you are the one inflicting the pain on yourself.*"

Bryant McGill

CHAPTER 7

Break the Ties to the Past

"Anger and resentment repressed, in illness will manifest"

~Penny Chiasson

W hy do doctors sometimes suggest events in your past are related to your pain? If you're like a lot of fibro conquerors, you've probably wondered what exactly does your past have to do with the pain you are having right now. Maybe you've even wondered if your doctors think you are crazy. Truth is, there's a lot of contributing relationship factors to fibromyalgia and chronic pain syndromes. In my experience with hundreds of hypnosis clients, almost all of us have past experiences we weren't able to address that weren't fair. Not fair equals anger. What I want to share with you is how forgiveness can help you begin a healing process. Surprised? Then you'll be even more surprised when you discover how all of this started much earlier than you imagined.

Anger is a poison

Laura was exhausted and lost because the focus she had on the direction of her life was gone. It began just after the death of her father. Laura's husband wanted to move to her childhood home. They had plans. Land in the mountains and designs for a dream home. This wasn't the plan. She had a business that was successful in New England. Would there be any chance of reaching her business goals and retiring from her job in rural America? Financial security and a meaningful life were important. She felt like she had thrown that away with the move.

This internal tension and uncertainty led to an almost life-ending spiral for Laura. She developed anxiety, which kept her up and going, sometimes 18 hours a day. Chronic back pain with severe episodes of myofascial pain syndrome made it difficult for her to work. Calling out was not an option. At least once a week, the exhaustion would weigh her down like a lead blanket, and she would pass out and sleep for hours. Her nurse practitioner put her on meds for mild depression and anxiety. It did not help.

Eventually, she was having emotional outbursts. Crying, anger, sometimes feeling like she wanted to explode. Especially on the days that she managed to sleep only two or three hours. She felt like she was going insane because she knew she had no reason to feel this way. Then one day, the emotional pain was too much. The thought of not being here would be less painful occurred to her. Terrified and overwhelmed that she would even think those kinds of thoughts, she called her nurse practitioner, who got her immediate professional help. After working with a therapist for a while, she got a referral so she could tackle her problem from the subconscious.

This journey is about you

When you began this journey, if you compared who you were when you started to who you desire to be, it seemed like a long trek. There are many steps to discovering your unique code. If you have been taking the small actions I have revealed to you, chances are you have noticed a difference. So have the people around you. The changes are subtle at first, then become a way of life. Now that you have found the peace in being compassionately detached when you choose to respond to circumstances in your life, it becomes easy to notice when you need to refocus that awareness.

You have probably noticed you have greater awareness around your relationships now, as well. Relationships cannot be avoided. Family, work, friends, and healthcare professionals might be just a few of the relationships you have. The journey that you are on is about you and for you. Just as with other aspects of the issues you deal with, they probably will not understand the time and effort you are investing. Too many people misunderstand chronic pain and cannot grasp that the sensation of physical pain created by the brain is very real. When you add other physical symptoms like extreme fatigue and brain fog, they give up understanding because they just don't get it.

Epigenetic expressions are more vulnerable to environmental and mental stress during the early period of life (including brief postnatal separation at birth). HOWEVER, the epigenome has a reversible property and can be potentially restored.[24]

Throughout this book, I have intentionally taken the focus off the symptoms and onto the desired outcome, because it is essential that I help you shift your focus. It has been my goal that you realize the small things that may have been aggravators that you can control. I bring your attention back here because as much as you would love for those around you to understand, they have no reference without experience. I've had the looks from coworkers when I arrived to work barely able to walk. The sideways glance when you grimace because you took a step, and it feels like a steel claw has gripped your back and shot lightening down your leg. A sensation so severe it takes your breath away. But you show up anyway.

No one can take your power unless you give it away

I am going to take you through a series of insights that will help you own your power. There are some things that you do just for you. Things that cannot ever be taken from you unless you allow it to happen.

Earlier in the book, I talked about perceptions. Not only do you have perceptions based on your life and reality, but so does everyone else. Their perceptions are loaded with all of the baggage of their life. You have begun a journey of releasing the past. They will still be stuck in theirs. Being compassionate with them, but detaching yourself from their baggage, is an important first step.

You are a work in progress. Be gracious to yourself because as you move forward on this journey, the road is not smooth. When you have a situation you are dealing with, and you are focused on responding instead of reacting to the circumstance, it may take more than you have at the moment to be compassionate with them. That is okay. Approach each situation independently, for what it is. Do your best, and move on.

Begin to take notice of your interactions with others. Don't shut them out because they don't understand. You have lived with the pain; they have not. Have gratitude that they have no point of reference. Because deep down inside, you don't want anyone to experience what you've gone through.

The second step is to understand that you always have been and always will be judged. How many times has someone judged you, and it made you angry or feel bad about yourself? It is human nature. Here is the golden nugget of judgment. When someone is judging you, it comes from what is inside of them. It is about their perceptions, their beliefs, their baggage, and their assumptions. It is not about you. This is so helpful in putting a degree of separation in your response. When you embrace that it is not about you, you become powerful.

How you choose to respond to someone who judges you is a reflection on you

When someone says or does something to you, or they judge you, and you become triggered, you are yourself judging. Judgment can be tied to a wide arrange of emotions, both positive and negative. When we are triggered, we are bringing all of our baggage of the past to the current situation, and it is mostly negative. If you find yourself feeling triggered *before responding* ask yourself, "What about this makes me feel triggered?"

Allow yourself to be honest here. You are the only one who hears the answer. Let me explain with an example. When your husband says you are using fibro as an excuse to be lazy, and you become triggered and angry, what about it made you angry? Is it more the fact that you have felt your life slipping through your fingers? That you feel out of control? That you are just so tired of the pain and didn't need to hear this? Is it simply hurting all the time? Deep down, you know he doesn't know what you go through, or maybe you are angry at what he said.

Taking the time to find precisely what is triggering you, so you can identify how you feel, gives you control. You can decide the best way to respond if you choose to respond at all. Compared to the greater whole of a day in your life, is it a response worth the currency of your time and health? Is it going to make a difference?

Pent up anger, guilt, and resentment we hold toward others and ourselves produce the same effect on the hypothalamus as stress. When we hold it in, the effects accumulate.[25]

If it is not going to make a difference, don't just stuff those emotions down like you have your entire life. Allow yourself a little privacy to feel them and let them go. If you find that it was some silly reason that you got triggered, and you were tired, and your mind was on autopilot, then dismiss the emotions. Sometimes we do experience emotions that are unnecessary because our subconscious responded based on past perceptions or misunderstandings. It's okay to just let those go.

Reframe to gain understanding

On this short journey, it is unrealistic and impossible to talk about all of the possible scenarios in relationships. One tactic that can help defuse a situation is meeting people where they are. If your husband is frustrated because you are tired and aren't helping out as much, you meet him where he is by saying, "If I were you I would be frustrated too. I understand you have to carry part of my load." Then you move him to where you need him to be by saying, "I am frustrated too, I want the energy to do the things I enjoy, I miss taking the kids to practice, etc."

If you had no idea what the fatigue and fog of fibro felt like, you would feel like your husband because you would have no point of reference. If you were him, you would be frustrated. He might have concerns about intimacy or health. This is a basic way to open up the lines of communication. You can't fix what you don't know needs fixing. Without communication, there can be no understanding.

The Holy Grail of Internal Peace

If you truly want internal peace, forgiveness is the key. As long as you hold onto past wrongs, whether they are based in reality or misperception, you have no control. These feelings, patterns, and beliefs began forming the moment you were born. Your mind will continue to run these programs subconsciously. This impacts your confidence, self-esteem, coping, and healing. These programs running under the surface create internal stress in the subconscious.

"Early life events, including physical trauma and psychosocial stressors influence gene expression, and the occurrence of fibromyalgia…this includes pain sensitivity changes resulting from premature birth, physical and sexual abuse."[26]

It seems pretty far-fetched, I know, but it's true. These subconscious beliefs and patterns affect how you perceive the world around you. This influences your overall sense of well-being. Your subconscious is on constant alert to protect you. If the subconscious is hypervigilant to protect you based on past perceptions, your stress response is easily activated over the smallest things. The body and mind go into fight or flight. The yang is on constant alert. The body grows weary. It adapts in an attempt to maintain readiness, and in its efforts, disease is created. Release the stress, and the Yin and Yang can return to a balanced state that supports the body's natural healing abilities.

When it comes to the past, we can forgive, or live and let live on a conscious level. In my experience, that is just avoiding facing the issue. True forgiveness requires getting into those underlying beliefs and feelings about a situation to achieve complete forgiveness. It allows for insight to occur so the anger can be released.

Release the rage

There are many ways to achieve this release. You can write a letter expressing the emotion and then burn it, see a counselor, or find a professional hypnotist experienced in modern, advanced techniques. As a 5-PATH® hypnotist, I am specially trained to guide clients through emotional release and forgiveness.

Together, Laura and I uncovered a misperception of being alone as a child that had affected her underlying sense of safety and security. Throughout her life, Laura had to make conscious efforts to come out of shyness and into her success. She finally felt like she had arrived. Then successive illnesses occurred with the death of her stepmother, followed by her father. During the period of illness, her stepmother gloated that she had intentionally hidden the severity of Laura's father's illness. Laura felt robbed of the opportunity to be at her father's side and make arrangements to be available to care for him as much as possible during his last two years.

With initial insight work, she resolved the misperceptions and erroneous fears around safety and security. Laura felt some improvement, but she still felt lost. As we moved to the next phase of the process, we released the anger and resentment Laura felt as a result of her stepmother's deception. Laura poured it all out. In a hypnotic state, Laura told her just what she thought. She cried. She yelled. She called her a "f**king b***ch." She did not stop until there was no anger left in her body. With the anger released, we began a process of insight, where deep down she was able to forgive her stepmother for what she had done.

Two days later, when we met for our final session, Laura informed me her life had taken a 180-degree turn after that session. Four sessions, and she was clear, focused, and committed to once again open a successful business. Three months later, her nurse practitioner reluctantly agreed to begin tapering her depression and anxiety medications. Six months later, she was off all medication, sleeping well, moving comfortably, and getting on with life.

You just discovered how your past could influence your relationships because feelings resonate. However, a word of warning – you aren't going to be 100 percent successful all the time in shifting your responses when you become frustrated or angry. So, first of all, I want you to have some grace with yourself and have pride in the effort you are making. That's because the key is that you need to take action on 1) identifying your triggers, 2) what about that particular situation makes you feel triggered, and 3) address the underlying cause. The sooner you do this, the sooner you'll be full in your power!

*If you have been diagnosed with a mental health condition, obtain your doctor's approval before seeking out hypnosis services.

Move Forward!

Who is one person you need to forgive so you can move on? Write that letter now, letting them know how you feel. Allow yourself to feel those emotions, then forgive and set yourself free.

"Two hours a week spent in nature is the key threshold for health and well-being — even those with long term illness and disability."

University of Exeter in Scientific Reports

CHAPTER 8

Use your Power to Recreate your Life

In the first seven chapters, we focused on what happens in our internal state that influences our physical world. Our internal dialogue creates unrecognized stress within our bodies and without. Observing your internal dialogue reveals surprising ways that it affects you and your interactions with the world around you, from self-love to conversations with strangers.

As you begin implementing techniques like thought-stopping and choosing to remain in silence rather than react to judgment and criticism, you may experience something called disintegration anxiety. No, you won't need a prescription for this. It is just the subconscious mind making you feel uncomfortable because you are no longer staying stuck in your old patterns. Even when it is a known harmful habit or behavior (like smoking or drinking, for example), the subconscious mind interferes when we consciously disrupt a pattern it has recognized as the status quo. For the subconscious, the status quo equals safety, even when it is harmful to us. After consistency in practicing thought-stopping, shifting negative thoughts to positive, and staying in your power, the subconscious will recognize this new way of being and accept it.

At this point, you are probably asking about all of the other things you have heard may cause or aggravate fibro like diet, exercise, and vitamin or mineral deficiencies. If you're like a lot of fibro conquerors, you've probably wondered, "Is this coincidence?" Maybe you've even wondered, "Is it true, or just a suggestion to shut us up?" The truth is, there's a lot of contradictory and outright confusing information floating around about how what we put into our body affects our health at the epigenetic level. That's why I reviewed the research and highlighted the most common findings here.

What we discovered is that your genetic code, the response you have to your environment, and what you put in your body is going to be unique. Surprised?

Then you'll be even more surprised when you discover there is no single road map, and the information is so vast it is difficult for doctors to keep up.

Moving forward, it's time to take a look at other pieces of the Fibro Code. The first step in deciding which may apply to you is developing an awareness of how you feel mentally, physically, and emotionally in external aspects. Armed with this information, you can decide where you want to focus your efforts to start.

Track your daily habits

Begin to track your daily habits. I know it can be a challenge to add something else to your plate. This is a big deal. Small actions, applied with consistency, yield big results. That is why you are here. I have made it as easy as possible. Head over to www.thefibrocode.com/resources and get your free tracking sheet right now. It has the essentials you need to track. You can make copies to keep in a notebook. It may take two or more weeks to notice any patterns, but the information will be the key to breaking your code.

It is important, first of all, to keep track of your comfort and energy levels throughout the day. The tracker uses a 0 to 5 scale, and a '0' represents no comfort or no energy at all, with 5 being the best you can feel. Also, while tracking these levels, make note of what activities you engage in each day. Even if it is only household activities, make a note. We are looking for trends in daily life where you can adjust and make things better.

Sleep habits

Tracking hours of sleep is also important. Too much or too little sleep are associated with increased health risks. The body needs 5-6 hours of sleep to activate healing and replenish hormone levels in the brain that tells our body we're satisfied with what we have eaten. If you are not sleeping well, you may find you are hungry all the time. 5-6 hours of sleep is also key to memory formation. Deep sleep is required for the brain to signal the body to engage in healing. Excessive sleepiness or daytime sleepiness should be addressed with your doctor. Distinguish between daytime sleepiness and fatigue. Knowing the difference will help your doctor when you share this information with them.

"The act of sleeping is a critical health behavior." [27]

Learning habits of good sleep hygiene may help you in your efforts to fall asleep easily and stay asleep. These include going to bed at the same time every night. Only sleeping in bed. No TV, eating, knitting, reading, or Facebooking on the phone in bed. The brain can associate bed with activities you have used to distract from not feeling well in the past rather than sleep. As a result, the brain can associate your bed with stimulation rather than sleep.

Food and Fibromyalgia

Food is a huge factor in inflammation, overall nutrition, energy, and gut health. The intricacies of nutrition and The Fibro Code go far beyond my knowledge, but I want to get you started. In the tracker download, I provide some resources for you to explore.

How many servings of fresh fruit and vegetables do you get? The more color, the better. Color means they have chemicals and nutrients that the body uses to fight inflammation, provide antioxidants, and support enzyme function. If you cannot afford fresh fruits and vegetables, flash-frozen vegetables packaged in bags in the freezer section of your grocery store are the next best option.

Do you eat a lot of starches, sugar, and bread? A high carb meal or snack without protein can result in sleepiness and fatigue when sugar levels crash. How many times have you had a sweet snack for energy, then crashed? It feels terrible. Sugary drinks and diets high in refined carbs (the processed stuff) are associated with inflammation.

Healthy protein helps you to feel satisfied and maintain blood sugar levels. (You don't get a surge of insulin when you eat protein. It is this surge with sugars that causes the carb crash.) When you have the opportunity, eat fish. Fish like salmon have oils that contain healthy omegas that support your immune system and fight inflammation. According to Harvard University, farm-raised salmon have similar Omega 3 fatty acid levels of wild-caught.

Water intake is the number one thing you can do for your body. Unless you are on a fluid restriction by your doctor, you should be drinking half of your body weight in ounces of water every day. So if you are 200 pounds, you should be drinking 100 ounces of water. Inadequate water intake impacts your body's efficiency in maintaining temperature regulation, enzyme function, acid-base balance, lubrication, and shock-absorbing fluids. The body cannot derive enough water from food or non-water beverages to meet this demand. The body uses hormones affecting blood concentration and kidney function to keep the delicate balance. The best thing you can do for your body is drink water. It can take several days of drinking water for your body's hormone balance to adjust and you feel a difference.

Avoid processed foods and artificial sweeteners. Buy organic when you can. Chemicals we introduce into the body that do not occur in nature can disrupt our body function at the cellular level. We don't know which of these chemicals or how much it takes to have a negative effect. Consider this: Europe has banned many of the chemicals we put into our foods and our skincare products due to health effects. Skin is your largest organ and absorbs chemicals we put on it. A simple GOOGLE search will yield many examples. What you put "in" your body includes more than food and drink!

Supplements

Taking vitamin and mineral supplements may be beneficial. Do so on the recommendation of your doctor, physician assistant, or nurse practitioner. Keep track of how you feel after starting. Magnesium, Vitamin D 3, and Vitamin B 12 are just a few that are found to be beneficial. Melatonin may be an option for inability to fall asleep. The following have had positive results in clinical trials in pain, tender points, stiffness, fatigue, and overall well-being: 5-HTP, Acetyl-l-carnitine, coenzyme q10, CoQ10 with Gingko Biloba, Collagen Hydrolysat, and s-adenosyl-L-Methionine.[2829] Over the counter vitamins, minerals, and supplements vary in their potency because they are not regulated by the FDA in the same way as prescribed medications. Find a reliable brand and stay with it.

Chemicals create internal "stress"

Eliminating chemicals can also improve how you feel. For example, 20 years ago, I worked in a major teaching hospital in Hartford, CT, in the ICU. One of the neurologists pleaded with the nurses to stop drinking diet beverages. Aspartame, a.k.a. Nutrasweet® crosses the blood-brain barrier. We still do not know exactly how anesthetics work, likewise we do not know exactly how aspartame affects the brain.

In 2010, a case report by Ciappuccini, et.al, describes two persons diagnosed with fibromyalgia syndrome, resistant to a spectrum of medications, and experiencing full remission after abstaining from aspartame.[30] Both patients had been diagnosed and treated by a rheumatologist. One of the patients voluntarily resumed aspartame with a full return of symptoms. The symptoms once again resolved when aspartame was eliminated again. The second refused to resume aspartame consumption and remained in remission.

Endocrine-disrupting chemicals like tobacco, air pollutants, solvents, metals, pesticides, flame retardants, non-stick chemicals, phthalates, and bisphenol A have been shown to play a role in the development of neurodevelopment disorders (specifically autism spectrum disorders) through possible epigenomic modifications.

Not all chemicals cross the blood-brain barrier. Chemicals and drugs that do alter the environment around the cells. Daily low-level exposure to chemicals could possibly lead to the gradual onset of symptoms. When we are exposed to environmental chemicals, we rarely factor them into the way we feel. We need to think about it. Consider making a list of all chemicals you use on a regular basis from non-stick cooking spray and aspartame to pesticides. Begin eliminating what you can live without.

Movement is important

Loving your body with movement is very beneficial when dealing with chronic pain. When chronic pain results in an inability to engage in physical activity, even for a very short period of time, muscles, ligaments, and tendons begin to shorten. Gently stretch your arms and legs. Even if it is only to walk from one end of the house to the other, once an hour, it is incredibly important to continue moving. Ask your doctor what is appropriate for you. If you have a physical disability, a physical therapist can teach you gentle exercises to maintain function. *If some degree of movement is not maintained, when feeling better, it takes very little activity to stretch the muscles and cause discomfort.* This can create a vicious cycle of pain, inactivity, decreased muscle function, increased pain, increased inactivity, inability to function.

Track the effect weather has on your comfort and sleep. Does humidity affect your comfort? What about storms or cold weather? Once you identify the patterns, you can watch the weather and *be proactive*. Take measures to create the highest level of comfort and function you can achieve during weather that has affected you negatively in the past. If you suffer headaches, allergies, or asthma, watch the weather and pollen count. When your allergies spiral out of control, your body goes into an inflammatory state. Increased inflammation equals increased discomfort. Be aware, be proactive.

Track changes in your medications and dosages. You intentionally take medications that cross the blood-brain barrier. That is how medications that improve depression, pain, nausea, Parkinson's, dementia — the list goes on — work. Live human testing on what is happening at the cellular level in the brain during exposure to medications and chemicals cannot be done. That is why side effects and adverse reactions vary with medications. It is dependent on your unique makeup, and study groups are limited to participants who meet very specific criteria for results to be valid.

Track medication changes

When adding new medications, make a note. *Don't look for the side effects.* The simple expectation of a side effect can create them within the subconscious. Instead, continue your regular daily tracking. If you notice a difference in how you feel, review what you have changed recently. When you include this information in your tracker along with any changes in energy, comfort, sleep, or other effects, your doctor or nurse practitioner can make better-informed decisions in your care.

Points mentioned here have been recognized in research to have an impact on areas such as inflammation, fatigue, activating stress, nervous system function, and physical conditioning. It is a lot of information. Do NOT try to overhaul and implement all of this at once. **The first priority is to begin to track *where you are now.***

If you have identified something you want to change, I recommend that you choose three small things you can change. Tie these changes to a current habit. For example, if you want to increase your water intake, and move just a little more, set a timer on your phone for every hour. When the hour is up, take the short stroll around the house or office, stopping into the kitchen to drink eight ounces of water. That's it. Do that for 21 days. Then take another item you want to address and add that. As you add new habits, I recommend using a habit tracker on your cell phone. It tracks your progress and lets you set reminders. Remember, start small and add to your routine. If you do too much at once, disintegration anxiety can kick in. Too much, too soon makes it difficult when it does not have to be.

If it is difficult to see yourself following through on implementing new habits, I recommend following through with the Breaking the Fibro Code companion guide. In the companion guide you get access to checklists that will aid you in deciphering this part of your code. Use the self-hypnosis and visualization exercises to create the new you that you are choosing to be!

"Healing is not healed.
Numbed is not healed.
Healing takes time.
Healing takes patience.
Healing takes love.
Healing sometimes triggers anger or sadness or sorrow or guilt or
regret.
Long suppressed.
Long unaddressed
So we make up that healing is wrong, useless and to be avoided
And we head back to numbing
And look for love and connection
With the numbed and suppressed, unaddressed and repressed...
Give space for the damage
Give space for the healing
Let the healing begin and begin and begin....."

Dave Rudbarg

CHAPTER 9

A Queen's Tale

C an your mind eliminate pain? If you're like a lot of chronic pain sufferers, you've probably wondered that if the brain created pain, then can the brain eliminate pain? Maybe you've even asked if pain eliminated using hypnosis and other techniques wasn't really pain. The truth is, there's a lot of contradictory and false information floating around about mind-body techniques to eliminate pain and untruths insinuating that people who find relief through mind-body techniques were not hurting.

After I personally experienced the power of the mind to block pain, I knew this was where all my years of training had led me to be. As I researched and expanded my knowledge, I discovered there are entire university psychology and neurobiology departments dedicated to learning how to use the mind to eliminate pain and suffering. Surprised? Read on to find out how one of my clients spontaneously eliminated chronic disabling pain when she had hypnosis sessions for confidence and motivation.

Patiently, I listened as Stormy started to tell me why she made an appointment with me. She was only three or four sentences in as she began to tear up. Stormy has a young, teenage daughter who wants her mother to show up in life. She says her daughter is why she is here. A lack of motivation and confidence in her ability to be a good mother was affecting her whole life. From finding the energy to get out of bed in the morning, to getting through the pain, to having a tidy home that her daughter is not embarrassed of.

Stormy is representative of so many of today's women. She was in her early 40s and a single mother trying to hold together a safe, stable, and nurturing home for her daughter. She also deals with chronic pain, as if her emotional strain and pain were not enough. Having been to several doctors and therapists, she had just accepted this was the way life had to be.

As she told me her story, my heart went out to Stormy. She listed off many events in her life that she believed affected her. Several of these events caused a great deal of shame and guilt. She believed these were the root of all her problems. She believed she didn't deserve a good life. She believed she was paying a punishment for past mistakes. I saw in Stormy her heart. She had a huge heart hidden under the weight of her past.

The more she talked, the tears began flowing in racking sobs. I gently tucked a tissue into her hand and let her express what needed expressing. In my experience, I have found that even though a client is with me for a hypnosis session, the most powerful thing I can do is be a compassionate listener.

Eventually, Stormy reached the point that I needed to intervene immediately to give her relief. Using her emotion, I guided her to a place where she could give herself some peace and insight. A place where she could show some love and compassion to herself. She wanted to learn 7th Path Self Hypnosis ®, so I wrapped up the hypnosis part of the session by anchoring the first recognition and having her practice taking herself back into hypnosis.

She was exhausted from the emotional outpouring. I encouraged her to be kind to herself by relaxing the rest of the day and drinking plenty of water. She left looking forward to our next session.

Stormy's insight work continued for the next two sessions. She was showing up with a smile on her face, which was something she said she had not done in a long time. Throughout the process, she began to see the events in her life from a new perspective. The events did not change, nor did the people. However, she took responsibility for the way she would allow the past to influence the way she felt from that day forward. With each session, she received a new recognition in 7th Path Self Hypnosis ® allowing her to continue the work on her own between our sessions.

When Stormy came in for her third session, I met her at the reception desk, as usual, to show her back. I noted that she did not have her cane for "just in case," and she was walking normally. She reported how she was feeling in the pre-hypnosis talk. I asked her about her walking. She was so excited that she almost shouted that she had not had any pain since our last session together. It was something she had been living with for a few years. I explained to her that sometimes our body can harbor emotional pain and distress in the body as physical pain. It is not something I can predict, but I was not surprised by how great she was feeling physically.

The fourth and fifth sessions would prove pivotal in her journey as well. There is a reason for the systematic approach I use. It allows for the peeling away of the layers of the past that provides insight at every level. Even though we were only halfway through, by the fourth session, she had lost ten pounds without trying. She said she enjoyed drinking water and was moving so much more now that she was pain-free. Another unexpected benefit!

We moved into another level of emotional release in these sessions. There is a reason I call forgiveness the "holy grail of internal peace." When we allow all of the pain of past wrongs and hurt to be expressed in a safe way, insight can occur. This insight can shift perceptions in a way that forgiveness happens on a level so deep it can allow a complete release of the past.

This forgiveness is not for the person(s) who hurt Stormy. It is for her. Setting her free of the chains of the past that kept her stuck in anger and resentment. It set her free of the erroneous belief that she needed to understand "why." At this point, all that mattered was her future. Stormy had taken her power back.

She was ready to mend her relationship with her mother. With hindsight, she allowed her subconscious mind to experience insight after releasing the anger. In therapy and her own private conversations with herself, she had tried to reason why she grew up with a mother who was beaten, and who stayed with a husband who had molested her half-sister for many years. Within the forgiveness process, she realized that she always knew deep down her mother was keeping them off the streets by staying with this awful man until she had means to leave. Seeing her mother from the perspective of doing her best, during the worst part of her own life, Stormy was able to forgive her mom for her childhood experiences.

Forgiveness is not only for others but for ourselves as well. That was the final step in our process on Stormy's journey to emotional freedom. When she arrived for this sixth and final session, she reported that for the first time in her life, when she lies down at night, her mind is quiet. She had fully incorporated daily self-hypnosis practice into her life and truly appreciated the difference it had made.

We completed her journey with me that day. Stormy was optimistic, motivated, and ready to make some significant changes in her life. She was contemplating adventures she had only dreamed of because she had lost all faith that it was meant to be in her life.

Even though we weren't targeting Stormy's discomfort or weight, those issues were tied closely together. While this is not uncommon when doing subconscious work, it cannot be predicted. Stormy also experienced insights that left her feeling significantly shifted at the end of the sessions. Sometimes it was a subtle shift, with an increased awareness of a new outlook on life. By focusing on what was most important to Stormy, and what she perceived to be her biggest problem, I was able to guide her on a journey of self-discovery. When she left that day, I was humbled and grateful for the opportunity to be a part of her transformation.

"Healing may not be so much about getting better, as about letting go of everything that isn't you – all of the expectations, all of the beliefs – and becoming who you are."

– Rachel Naomi Remen

CHAPTER 10

A Lifetime of Healing

C an all pain be eliminated using the power of the mind? You've probably wondered about all the testimonials and comments you see on websites and Facebook posts regarding immediate and complete elimination of pain. Maybe you've even wondered if it's all hype. The truth is that clients respond along a spectrum of results. It cannot be predicted who gets that complete and total elimination. Because it can and does happen, those testimonials are used to create subconscious expectations of the possibility. It improves results.

The one question I ask my clients is, "What will life be like 30%, 50%, 75%, and 100% more comfortable." It allows us to build our partnership in truth. Not everyone receives 100% relief. However, life becomes more livable, enjoyable, and successful when you are in control. Keep reading to learn more about Gina. She has taken her journey to comfort and integrated her experience of overcoming struggle to help women launch successful coaching careers. Gina has even become trained in hypnosis.

Our subconscious mind operates off emotion. Even before we can voice what we are feeling, the unconscious generates feelings dependent on the subconscious' interpretation of our sense of safety, security, and fair/not fair. We weren't born all-knowing. The mind identifies patterns of behavior and emotion, and it tends to favor those behaviors that contribute to a feeling of safety. These patterns in the context of our environment at the time form our beliefs.

These beliefs form without our conscious awareness. The mind, with repetition, becomes conditioned and hard-wired through a process known as neuroplasticity. When we get caught in a cycle of pain and can't see a way out, the brain can hard-wire these beliefs in a way that is difficult to remember. A doctor can tell you that you will have to live with the pain for the rest of your life, and being in a more suggestible state with a person of authority, it can influence you on a subconscious level. Even if you don't want it and consciously don't believe it, you can be affected on a deeper level. These beliefs and thoughts associated with them can create a vicious cycle that amplifies pain.

It's not conscious. No one chooses to have these beliefs. Then one day awareness occurs. "How did I end up in this place?" "If I knew then what I know now, boy, I would have done things differently!" That's why we often say that hindsight is 20/20. These beliefs are not permanent, though. Our beliefs can shift with life events. We can choose to change our thoughts, and with repetition, hard-wire our new beliefs. We can create a new reality—one that is in our best interest.

It had been almost six years since the accident. Gina and I connected in 2014 and started working together for the relief of her pain. Shortly after we got started, life got in the way, and other priorities required her attention. Now she was looking back at me from over 1,000 miles away telling me she finally found a doctor who properly diagnosed her with Chronic Regional Pain Syndrome (CRPS). Gina appeared pale, tired, and mentally exhausted from all that life was throwing at her.

Even though Gina refused to be defeated, she seemed to be unsure where to begin to find relief. It was at this point that I let Gina know that hypnosis was an effective option for CRPS. We discussed what an optimal plan would look like and what she could expect. Gina's CRPS had severely hampered any progress with physical therapy. Once her pain was reduced or eliminated, she could once again work to increase the function of her shoulder. I informed Gina she might experience discomfort when progressing in her PT as she strengthened and lengthened her muscles, ligaments, and tendons. There was no need to fear this discomfort because it was a discomfort of progress.

Fear of pain can be more painful than the pain itself.

International Association for the Study of Pain

Gina scheduled to work specifically on her chronic pain. Her journey started a little different than Stormy's. With prior commitments, it was difficult to meet once a week, much less more often. Because of this, Gina wanted to use 7th Path Self Hypnosis ® to facilitate clearing any negativity right away. After a few weeks of using 7th Path and observing her internal dialogue, Gina had come to the realization of how much her emotions and past were playing a role in her discomfort. She was ready to dig into the deep work.

Living with chronic pain affects every aspect of your life, from how you feel about your day to taking your kids out to play. Thoughts and realizations begin to impact how you view your world and future. These feelings can resonate with the past, amplifying your discomfort, and affecting your sense of well-being. You don't even realize it. Before you know it, your subconscious mind has created a new normal. This occurs through neuroplasticity, which we discussed earlier.

Gina made a conscious effort to change the way she talked to herself. From the first time we met years earlier, she had eliminated the word "pain" from her vocabulary. It is an important first step because we have beliefs and expectations surrounding the word "pain." She decided to be more conscious of what she said to herself and shifted her thoughts if she realized they were becoming negative. Gina began to make progress because she was consistent in her efforts.

With determination and courage, Gina was ready to let go of the past so that she could embrace the future. She had a childhood typical of many of my clients who had lived with chronic pain. It was not abusive or mean, but the family dynamic created situations where she felt alone and afraid at a very young age. These situations repeated themselves in her early years. It created stress in her young mind.

Research suggests that stress during early life and the formative years can result in epigenetic changes associated with chronic pain, especially fibromyalgia.

Even though Gina was not alone, and there was no need to be afraid, her subconscious had created this belief. 5-PATH® is a process that gave her the opportunity to recognize with a deep understanding that she was safe, secure, and loved, even when daddy was napping, and mom was at work. At other times in her life, these same beliefs had played out, and she began to look at them in a new light. These subconscious shifts in belief had a significant effect on Gina's outlook. Before that moment, her perspective had been through the subconscious lens of fear.

Gina continued through the process. She was making progress with physical therapy, back in the water, doing mild resistance training to regain strength. Life continued to throw curveballs, but she refused to back down. Going through the process of forgiveness was a tough one. Like many women, society had impressed upon her that it is not ladylike to be angry. Pretty is as pretty does. Sound familiar? What we get in return for not acknowledging our feelings and moving on is subconscious tension from unfinished business. With encouragement, she powered through the sessions, improving with each step in the process.

Every client has a moment that is pivotal for them. For Gina, this was when we used hypnosis to allow her to dialogue with the part of her that made decisions in the past that hurt her. Being embarrassed about the way she looked. Not standing up to coaches who were abusive and harsh, forcing her to play while injured. Eagerly seeking approval from the outside in, instead of the inside out.

Her most raw and vulnerable side came out in this session. It was a safe place for her to be honest with herself about a time in her life when she made a desperate cry for help to release her anger and frustration. She wanted to reach a deeper level of understanding that she did the best she could with what she knew at the time, and in that moment in the past, she didn't know how else to get her own attention to get help. This was pivotal for Gina, because deep inside, she had never moved on from this moment. It had defined her perspective of her past and herself. In this moment, she was able to gain insight, release her past, and love her true self.

The next time I saw Gina, she was glowing. Lighter. The shift was visible in her face and body language. At this point, Gina was comfortable 75-80% of the time, with only four days or so of significant discomfort. Using the self-hypnosis skills she learned along with other self-care strategies she had implemented, she could get these days under control. This was a great improvement from every day in pain and 75-80% of the day in significant pain. Gina was living fully again.

Sometime later, Gina had a family gathering to attend. While getting dressed and looking for something comfortable to wear, her pain came on strong. We spent some time talking about it and found that she did not like crowds because people would forget about her injury and grab her to hug her. A theme revealed itself where the discomfort would appear at times when she had plans to go out and be in groups of people. Using hypnosis, we released this fear. She also took this opportunity to create a strategy for when she was ready to go out in public.

After our last session together, Gina went through a challenging period with a change in doctors, followed by her mother's deteriorating health. Strengthened by everything she had learned about her body and its ability to heal, she was determined to find someone who could help her mother. Gina admits that it took consistently putting her own body and health first to be able to have the mental and physical energy to do what needed to be done to get help for her mother. In the end, it all paid off. Gina is growing her business and her health at the same time.

Not everyone who uses hypnosis for pain is going to have an immediate and complete end to their discomfort. Like Gina, for many, it can be weeks, months, or a life-long process. Gina has discovered that to be at her best, she must turn her attention to loving her body and giving it the attention it needs. What she has learned about herself allows her to serve others at a deeper level of understanding. She knows firsthand what it is to overcome diversity and excel. Through consistency, she continues to improve her life.

Creating health in your body is about looking at your mind, body, and soul. Look for the things you can change. Start small, making it manageable, and be consistent. Gina manages her diet, water intake, physical therapy, exercise, meditation, hot tub therapy, self-hypnosis, and protecting her energy by choosing who she spends time with. Making changes to everything at once creates stress in the subconscious. It challenges the status quo, which represents safety and security to the subconscious. She has incorporated these changes over time and now lives life fully again.

What's Next?

This is only the beginning. You may have picked up this book looking for answers with a quick fix. Oh, how I wish it were so. Your code is unique. The solution is within you. Some of the things you have learned can begin to have an immediate impact. Others must become a part of your life. They must become part of who you are. Honor yourself mentally, physically, and emotionally.

Many times, I talked about simple steps. I know that you have realized by now that simple does not mean easy. Always remember this as you continue your healing journey: you are not only worth it; you are worthy of it. When it feels like it is so far away, think about the one thing that you are passionate about and brings you joy. Feel that joy. It is connected to your purpose. If at times it feels you cannot do it for you, do it for your purpose.

Moving forward, read this book again and again. Each time you will find something new. You will learn something you weren't ready to learn the first time. Take each day one step at a time. Give yourself grace. Love yourself. It is this process of persistence with patience and love for yourself that will bring you the results you desire.

It is my desire that this book doesn't just make an impact on your physical healing, but also opens a doorway to your emotional freedom. We put what we love first in our lives. It's not selfish. It's benefitting those you wish to look after in your life. Ancient wisdom, philosophies, and even the Bible speak of making sure your own needs are met before taking care of others. Love yourself and put yourself first. You are enough. You deserve this. Embrace it.

If you have questions about what you have read, or you need detailed information to move through the recommendations in this book, the companion guide may be perfect for you. Each step is broken down into 7 days of repetition, and you can spend as long as you like in any section. You can also join the Facebook group, Breaking the Fibro Code, to be a part of a community that is looking beyond healthcare for the answers they need to heal. If you prefer a more interactive approach, you can find more information about ways to work with Penny at www.pennychiasson.com.

Acknowledgments

Writing this book has been a labor of love. It has taken me on a journey of awareness. It is more than understanding the lives of my reader on a much deeper level. I have to know what you are going through. As a part of this process, I immersed myself in online communities, asked questions and called upon my clinical experiences with patients who had fibromyalgia. I spent hours buried in research articles searching for answers. As a part of this process, I have had to gain a deeper understanding of myself and my knowledge and abilities. It has been more than the creation of a book; the process created a new me.

This book would not be in your hands without the expert assistance of Divya Parekh. She has been both patient and gently pushing throughout this process. On the days I felt that no one with fibromyalgia would give a damn about what I had to offer, she was there to lead me to the light. Divya would not even be a part of my journey as a healer had it not been for my friend Lisa Marie Pepe who connected us on an earlier project. Much gratitude and thanks to you both.

Friend, author, transformational soul and poet Jill Renee Stevens created the inspiration poem in the introduction and graciously permitted me to use it here. Many thanks to Flora Bailey who contributed her magnificent talent to create art through photography in my photo shoot.

My husband, Ron, has always stood by me and believed in me no matter how crazy my ideas seemed. Andrew, Thomas, and Michael were patient all those years with a mother who had no desire for domestication and spent so many years in school. My mother, Diane (who has seen a lot less of me this year than she deserves), is responsible for my lifelong passion to be and do more. For that, I am grateful.

I cannot end this book without mentioning my father, Sammy, and my grandparents, Evelyn, George, Sue, and Buster. I love you, and I can't wait to see you in the next leg of our Divine Journey.

1   Bonaz, B., and Sinneger, V., and Pellissier, S. Vagal Tone: effects on sensitivity, Motility, and inflammation. Neurogastroenterol Motil. 2016;28,455-462.

2   Hannibal, KE., and Bishop, MD. Chronic Stress Cortisol Dysfunction and Pain: A Psychoneuroendocrine Rationale for Stress Management in Pain Rehabilitation. Physical Therapy. 2014;94:1816-1825.

3   Mohd, R. Life Event, Stress and Illness. 2008;15(4):9-18.

4   Mohd, R. Life Event, Stress and Illness. 2008;15(4):9-18.

5   Kok, B., Coffey, K. et al. How Positive Emotions Build Physical Health: Perceived Positive Social Connections Account for the Upward Spiral Between Positive Emotions and Vagal Tone. Psychological Science. Accessed Online 2019.

6   Curtis, B., and O'Keefe, J. Autonomic Tone as a Cardiovascular Risk Factor: The Dangers of Chronic Fight or Flight Mayo Clin Proc. 2002;77:45-54

7   Curtis, B., and O'Keefe, J. Autonomic Tone as a Cardiovascular Risk Factor: The Dangers of Chronic Fight or Flight Mayo Clin Proc. 2002;77:45-54

8   Frokjer, J, Bergmann, S. et al. Modulation of vagal tone enhances gastroduodenal motility and reduces somatic pain sensitivity. Neurogastroenterol Motil. 2016;28,592-598.

9   Sedan, O., Sprecher, E., Yarnitsky, D. Vagal stomach afferents inhibit somatic pain perception. Pain. 2005;113,354-359.

10   Mohd, R. Life Event, Stress and Illness. 2008;15(4):9-18.

11   Janssen, S. Negative affect and sensitization to pain. Scandinavian Journal of Psychology. 2002;43,131-137.

12   Janssen, S. Negative affect and sensitization to pain. Scandinavian Journal of Psychology. 2002;43,131-137.

13   Janssen, S. Negative affect and sensitization to pain. Scandinavian Journal of Psychology. 2002;43,131-137.

14   McEwen, B., Eiland, L. et al. Stress and anxiety: Structural plasticity and epigenetic regulation as a consequence of stress. 2012;62(1)3-12.

15   Martarelli, D., Cocchioni, M., et al. Diaphragmatic Breathing Reduces Exercise-Induced Oxidative Stress. Evidence Based Complementary and Alternative Medicine. 2011.

16   Pavlov, V., and Tracey, K. Neural regulators of innate immune responses and inflammation. Cellular and molecular life sciences. 2004;61,2322-2331.

17   Baghdadi, G., and Nasrabadi, A. An Investigation of Changes in Brain Wave Energy During Hypnosis with Respect to Normal EEG. Sleep and Hypnosis. 2009;2:11.

18   Black, D., and Slavich, G. Mindfulness meditation and the immune system: a systematic review of randomized controlled trials. Accessed Online 2019.

19   Kanherkar, R., Stair, S. et al. Epigenetic Mechanisms of Integrative Medicine. Accessed Online 2019.

20   Zachariae, R. Psychoneuroimmunology: A Bio-psycho-social approach to health and disease. Scandanavian Journal of Psychology. 2009;50:645-651.

21   Guy Montgomery, PhD, Katherine DuHamel, PhD, and William Redd, PhD

22   Spiegel, H. Nocebo: The Power of Suggestibility. Preventive Medicine. 1997;26:616-621

23   Spiegel, H. Nocebo: The Power of Suggestibility. Preventive Medicine. 1997;26:616-621

24   Agnelli, S, Ardendt-Nielsen, L et al. Fibromyalgia: Genetics and epigenetics insights may provide the basis for the development of diagnostic biomarkers. Accessed Online 2019.

25   Mohd, R. Life Event, Stress and Illness. 2008;15(4):9-18.

26   Grander, M., and Patel, Nirav. Editorial; From sleep duration to mortality: implications of meta-analysis and future directions. J. Sleep Res. 2009;18:145-147.

27   Grander, M., and Patel, Nirav. Editorial; From sleep duration to mortality: implications of meta-analysis and future directions. J. Sleep Res. 2009;18:145-147.

28   Arranz, L., Canela, M., Rafecas, M. Fibromyalgia and Nutrition, what do we know?. Rheumatol Int. 2010;30:1417-1427.

29   Rossi, A., Lollo, A.C., et al. Fibromyalgia and nutrition: what news?. Clin Exp Rheumatol. 2015;33:s117-s125.

30   Ciappuccini, R., et. Al. Aspartame-induced fibromyalgia, an unusual but curable cause of chronic pain. Clinical and Experimental Rheumatology; 28 (suppl. 63):S131-S133

Made in the USA
Middletown, DE
19 February 2022